Mastering Primary English

Mastering Primary Teaching series

Edited by Judith Roden and James Archer

The *Mastering Primary Teaching* series provides an insight into the core principles underpinning each of the subjects of the Primary National Curriculum, thereby helping student teachers to 'master' the subjects. This in turn will enable new teachers to share this mastery in their teaching. Each book follows the same sequence of chapters, which has been specifically designed to assist trainee teachers to capitalize on opportunities to develop pedagogical excellence. These comprehensive guides introduce the subject and help trainees know how to plan and teach effective and inspiring lessons that make learning irresistible. Examples of children's work and case studies are included to help exemplify what is considered to be best and most innovative practice in primary education. The series is written by leading professionals, who draw on their years of experience to provide authoritative guides to the primary curriculum subject areas.

Also available in the series

Mastering Primary Languages, Paula Ambrossi and Darnelle Constant-Shepherd

Mastering Primary Music, Ruth Atkinson

Mastering Primary Physical Education, Kristy Howells with Alison Carney, Neil Castle and Rich Little

Mastering Primary Science, Amanda McCrory and Kenna Worthington

Forthcoming in the series

Mastering Primary Art and Design, Peter Gregory, Claire March and Suzy Tutchell

Mastering Primary Computing, Graham Parton and Christine Kemp-Hall

Mastering Primary Design and Technology, Gill Hope

Mastering Primary Geography, Anthony Barlow and Sarah Whitehouse

Mastering Primary History, Karin Doull, Christopher Russell and Alison Hales

Mastering Primary Mathematics, Andrew Lamb, Rebecca Heaton and Helen Taylor

Mastering Primary Religious Education, Maria James and Julian Stern

Also available from Bloomsbury

Developing Teacher Expertise, edited by Margaret Sangster

Readings for Reflective Teaching in Schools, edited by Andrew Pollard

Reflective Teaching in Schools, Andrew Pollard

Mastering Primary English

Wendy Jolliffe and David Waugh

BLOOMSBURY ACADEMIC
LONDON • NEW YORK • OXFORD • NEW DELHI • SYDNEY

BLOOMSBURY ACADEMIC
Bloomsbury Publishing Plc
50 Bedford Square, London, WC1B 3DP, UK
1385 Broadway, New York, NY 10018, USA

BLOOMSBURY, BLOOMSBURY ACADEMIC and the Diana logo are trademarks
of Bloomsbury Publishing Plc

First published 2018
Reprinted 2018

Cover design by Anna Berzovan
Cover image © iStock (miakievy/molotovcoketail)

A catalogue record for this book is available from the British Library.

Names: Jolliffe, Wendy, author. | Waugh, David (David G.)author.
Title: Mastering Primary English / Wendy Jolliffe and David Waugh.
Description: London ; New York : Bloomsbury Academic, An imprint of Bloomsbury
Publishing Plc, 2018. | Includes bibliographical references and index.
Identifiers: LCCN 2017051480| ISBN 9781474295468(hardback| ISBN 9781474295451(pbk.) |
ISBN 9781474295475 (ePDF) | ISBN 9781474295482 (ePub)
Subjects: LCSH: English language–Study and teaching(Primary) | English literature–
Study and teaching (Primary) | Language arts (Primary)
Classification: LCC LB1528 .J65 2018 | DDC 372.6–dc23
LC record available at https://lccn.loc.gov/2017051480

ISBN: HB: 978-1-4742-9546-8
PB: 978-1-4742-9545-1
ePDF: 978-1-4742-9547-5
ePub: 978-1-4742-9548-2

Series: Mastering Primary Teaching

Typeset by Deanta Global Publishing Services, Chennai, India
Printed and bound in Great Britain

To find out more about our authors and books visit www.bloomsbury.com
and sign up for our newsletters.

Contents

About the Authors   vi

Series Editors' Foreword   vii

How to Use This Book   x

Acknowledgements   xii

Introduction   **1**

1 **An Introduction to Primary English**   **5**

2 **Current Developments in Primary English**   **19**

3 **English as an Irresistible Activity:** Promoting Creativity
   in English   **33**

4 **English as a Practical Activity:** Being a Reader   **51**

5 **Skills to Develop in English:** The Four Modes of Language   **73**

6 **Children's Ideas:** Engaging Children with Writing   **107**

7 **Assessing Children in English**   **129**

8 **Practical Issues:** Challenges for Trainee and Beginner Teachers **145**

Bibliography   167

Index   179

About the Authors

Wendy Jolliffe

Wendy is Professor of Education and was, until recently, Head of Teacher Education at the University of Hull, UK. She has worked as a regional adviser for ITT for the National Strategies and advised ITT providers on effective provision for literacy. Wendy is a former deputy headteacher in a primary school in Hull and she has published extensively on teaching English and implementing cooperative learning.

David Waugh

David is Associate Professor and subject leader for Primary English at Durham University, UK. He has published extensively in primary English. David is a former deputy headteacher, was Head of the Education department at the University of Hull, UK, and was a regional adviser for ITT for the National Strategies from 2008 to 2010. As well as his educational writing, David also writes children's stories, including *Lottie's Run, 'Girls Can't Play Football!', Jessica's Other World* and *The Wishroom,* a novel written with forty-five children from fifteen East Durham schools.

Series Editors' Foreword

Long and varied experience of working with beginning and experienced teachers in primary schools has informed this series since its conception. Over the last 30 years there have been many changes to practice in terms of teaching and learning in primary and early years education. Significantly, since the implementation of the first National Curriculum in 1989, the aim has been to bring best practice in primary education to all state schools in England and Wales. As time has passed, numerous policy changes have altered the detail and emphasis of the delivery of the primary curriculum. However, there has been little change in the belief that in the primary and early years phases of education, pupils should receive a broad balanced curriculum based on traditional subjects.

Recent Ofsted subject reports, and notably the Cambridge Primary Review, indicate that rather than the ideal being attained, in many schools, the emphasis on English and mathematics has not only depressed the other subjects of the primary curriculum, but also narrowed the range of strategies used for the delivery of the curriculum. Provision in the amount of time allocated to subject sessions in ITE courses has dramatically reduced which may also account for this narrow diet in pedagogy.

The vision of this series of books was borne out of our many years of experience with student teachers. As a result, we believe that the series is well designed to equip trainee and beginning teachers to master the art of teaching in the primary phase. This series of books aims to introduce current and contemporary practices associated with the whole range of subjects within the Primary National Curriculum and religious education. It also goes beyond this by providing beginning teachers the knowledge and understanding required to achieve mastery of each subject. In doing so, each book in the series highlights contemporary issues such as assessment and inclusion which are key areas that even the most seasoned practitioner is still grappling with in light of the introduction of the new primary curriculum. As a result, equipped with these texts we believe that students who work in schools and progress onto their NQT year will be able to make a significant contribution to the provision in their school, especially in foundation subjects.

Readers will find great support within each one of these texts. Each book in the series will inform and provide the opportunity for basic mastery of each of the subjects,

English, mathematics, science, physical education, music, history, geography, design and technology computing and religious education. Readers can expect to learn much about each of the subjects in the series. They will discover the essence of each subject in terms of its philosophy, knowledge and skills. Readers will also be inspired by the enthusiasm for each subject revealed by the subject authors who are experts in their field. They will discover many and varied strategies for making each subject 'come alive' for their pupils and they should become more confident about teaching across the whole range of subjects represented in the primary and early years curriculum.

Primary teaching in the state sector is characterized by a long history of pupils being taught the whole range of the primary curriculum by one teacher. Although some schools may employ subject specialists to deliver some subjects of the curriculum, notably physical education, music or science for example, it is more usual for the whole curriculum to be delivered to a class by their class teacher. This places a potentially enormous burden on beginning teachers no matter which route they enter teaching. The burden is especially high on those entering through employment-based routes and on those who aim to become inspiring primary teachers. There is much to learn!

The term 'mastery' is generally considered to relate to knowledge and understanding of a subject which incorporates the 'how' of teaching as well as the 'what'. Although most entrants to primary teaching will have some experience of the primary curriculum as pupils, very few will have any understanding of the kind of broad curriculum which reflects recent trends in teaching and learning within the subject. The primary curriculum encompasses a very broad range of subjects each of which has its own knowledge base, skills and ways of working. Unsurprisingly, very few new entrants into the teaching profession hold mastery of all the interrelated subjects. Indeed for the beginning teacher it may well be many years before full mastery of all aspects of the primary curriculum is achieved. The content of the primary curriculum has changed significantly, notably in some foundation subjects such as history and music. So although beginning teachers might hold fond memories of these subjects from their own experience of primary education, the content of the subject may well have changed significantly over time and may incorporate different emphases.

The title of the series, Mastering Primary Teaching, aims to meet the needs of those who, reflecting the desire for mastery of each subject, want to know more. This is a tall order. Nevertheless we believe that the pursuit of development should always be rewarded which is why we are delighted to have so many experts sharing their well-developed knowledge and passion for the subjects featured in each text. The vision for this series was to provide support for those who are beginning their teaching career that may not feel fully secure in their subject knowledge, understanding and skill. In addition the vision was to provide a reference point for beginning teachers to always be able to go back to support them in the important art of teaching.

Intending primary teachers, in our experience, have a thirst for knowledge about the subject that they will be teaching. They want to 'master' new material and ideas in a range of subjects. They aim to gain as much knowledge as they can of the subjects they will be teaching, some of which they may be unfamiliar with, lacking in confidence about or, quite frankly, scared to death because of their perceived lack of familiarity with some subjects and particularly how they are delivered in primary schools. Teaching the primary curriculum can be one of the most rewarding experiences. We believe that this series will help you to unlock the primary curriculum in a way that sees you establish yourself as a confident primary practitioner.

Judith Roden
James Archer
June 2017

How to Use This Book

This book is one of twelve books that together help form a truly innovative series that is aimed to support your development. Each book follows the same format and chapter sequence. There is an emphasis throughout the book on providing information about the teaching and learning of English. You will find a wealth of information within each chapter that will help you to understand the issues, problems and opportunities that teaching the subject can provide you as a developing practitioner in the subject. Crucially, each chapter provides opportunities for you to reflect upon important points linked to your development in order that you may master the teaching of English. As a result you too develop your confidence in the teaching of primary English. There really is something for everyone within each chapter.

Each chapter has been carefully designed to help you to develop your knowledge of the subject systematically and as a result contains key features. Chapter objectives clearly signpost the content of each chapter and these will help you to familiarize yourself with important aspects of the subject and will orientate you in preparation for reading the chapter. The regular 'pause for thought' points offer questions and activities for you to reflect on important aspects of the subject. Each 'pause for thought' provides you with an opportunity to enhance your learning beyond merely reading the chapter. These will sometimes ask you to consider your own experience and what you already know about the teaching of the subject. Others will require you to critique aspects of good practice presented as case studies or research. To benefit fully from reading this text, you need to be an active participant. Sometimes you are asked to make notes on your response to questions and ideas and then to revisit these later on in your reading. While it would be possible for you to skim through the opportunities for reflection or to give only cursory attention to the questions and activities which aim to facilitate deeper reflection than might otherwise be the case, we strongly urge you to engage with the 'pause for thought' activities. It is our belief that it is through these moments that most of your transformational learning will occur as a result of engaging this book. At the end of each chapter, you will find a summary of main points from the chapter along with suggestions for further reading.

We passionately believe that learners of all ages learn best when they work with others, so we would encourage you, if possible, to work with another person, sharing your ideas and perspectives. This book would also be ideal for groups study within a university or school setting.

This book has been authored by Wendy Jolliffe and David Waugh, who are experienced and highly regarded as professionals in their subject area. They are strong voices within the primary English community. By reading this book you will be able to benefit from their rich knowledge, understanding and experience. When using this, ensure that you are ready to learn from some of the greats in primary English.

Acknowledgements

We are grateful to all the teachers and trainee teachers who provided ideas and experiences for case studies for this book. We are also grateful to the children and parents who allowed the examples of children's work to be included, and to the trainee teachers from Durham University who presented the work so beautifully. We would like to thank the schools which allowed us to photograph their displays for inclusion in the book. We are particularly grateful to staff at Sherburn Primary in Durham who allowed us to take photographs of their displays.

Introduction

This book explores how best to teach the primary curriculum programme of study for English so that it motivates children and secures their understanding of key aspects of developing the skills of speaking and listening, reading and writing. The book will be particularly useful for trainees on new and conventional routes into teaching, but will also support practising teachers.

Each chapter includes

- Lists of chapter objectives
- Case studies with questions
- Diagrams and figures
- Illustrations
- Conclusion and summaries
- Questions, reflections and activities
- Recommended further reading
- Extracts from current research and policy

In Chapter 1, what being 'literate' means is explored and how the four modes of language all interrelate to support this process. The chapter examines the challenges for teachers in helping children become literate, including meeting the demands of a changing curriculum, and the importance of basing teaching on research-validated principles. A key feature is an examination of the latest research findings, including those from the Education Endowment Foundation. How to support an increasing number of children who have English as an additional language is reviewed, with key factors to support them. Case studies of different approaches schools have taken in effective teaching of English help in exemplifying effective practice.

Chapter 2 looks at current developments in the teaching of primary English, exploring recent government policy directions and their impact on the teaching of English. The chapter focuses on developing readers' understanding of the concept of 'mastery' and considers how 'mastery' can relate to the teaching of English. It goes on to look at current developments in the teaching of English that support 'mastery', and provides an overview of research findings in the teaching of English related to developing mastery. Case studies are included in order to exemplify approaches to mastery.

Chapter 3 examines ways of promoting creativity in English and clarifies what is meant by creativity, providing a clear understanding of the features of creativity in the learning and teaching of English. There is a review of research studies that explore creative approaches, and the chapter shows how literature, drama, art, visual texts, film, technology and multimedia can act as a stimulus for creativity. Case studies of creative approaches used in schools illustrate strategies which readers might consider in their own classrooms.

Chapter 4 examines what it means to be a reader and how teachers can develop both their pupils' and their own reading skills and understanding. The chapter emphasizes the key role that teachers play, not only in teaching the basic skills of reading, but also in motivating children to become real readers who view reading as a valuable life skill and a source of pleasure. Through research and case studies it looks at ways of making reading an attractive and engaging activity for children, and stresses the importance of engaging children with poetry as well as stories, digital texts and non-fiction.

The skills involved in developing proficient speakers, listeners, readers and writers, the four modes of language, are examined in Chapter 5. Drawing upon research studies, the chapter analyses the elements of vocabulary, spelling, grammar and punctuation and how these can be taught in creative ways. Case studies of schools that are explicitly teaching the skills to exemplify developing mastery in contextualized ways are presented and discussed.

Chapter 6 explores ways of engaging children with writing. The chapter begins by looking at pupil performance in writing and gender differences. Different approaches to teaching and learning writing are then examined, including how grammar can be taught through writing, rather than through a discrete lesson. There is a strong emphasis on modelling writing for children, and on ways in which teachers can write with and for children. The chapter includes a case study of a novel written by a teacher with forty-five pupils from fifteen schools.

Chapter 7 looks at assessing children in English and examines the underlying rationale for different forms of assessment, with a focus on formative assessment, or assessment for learning. The chapter discusses the implications of assessment without levels and provides case studies to show how schools are developing new approaches to assessment in English. It also includes an exploration of peer and self-assessment.

Finally, Chapter 8 explores the challenges faced by trainee and beginner teachers, looking at identifiable qualities of effective teachers, with a particular focus on primary English. Through case studies, the chapter offers some practical solutions to challenges.

Our lengthy experience in primary education has afforded us opportunities to see thousands of examples of good practice and to reflect on this after reading research from around the world. We have drawn upon this experience to offer practical ideas for the classroom. If you are (and you certainly should be) keen to be the best teacher of primary English that you can be, there is no shortage of good practice and research which you can draw upon to help you develop your practice.

We show how teaching can be both creative and rigorous and discuss cooperative learning and mastery learning. We also emphasize the importance of modelling and of teachers' subject knowledge, as well as looking at what research tells us constitutes effective teaching. Consideration has also been given to ways of motivating and engaging children in learning. This book does not provide all the solutions to the challenges you will face as a teacher of primary English, but we hope you will use it as a starting point for enhancing your teaching and developing your pupils' learning.

English is at the heart of the primary curriculum and through engaging pupils with literacy and oracy we can open doors to the rest of the curriculum. We hope that through reading this book you will reflect on the practice you see in schools and on your own teaching.

Wendy Jolliffe
David Waugh
July 2017

Chapter 1
An Introduction to Primary English

Chapter objectives

This chapter will explore

- Conceptions about literacy
- The four modes of language and the importance of speaking and listening
- The challenges of the English language
- Cross-curricular approaches to teaching English
- The changing curriculum for English
- Research findings into improving literacy
- Supporting children who have English as an additional language

Literacy ... includes not only reading and writing as processes, but how individual minds and collective cultures are affected once these processes take hold.
Bruner (2002: 86)

Introduction

This chapter will begin by providing a broad look at literacy and what being literate entails. Frith (1998: 1051) argues, based on findings from neuroscience, that '*reading literally changes the brain*', as acquiring knowledge of the alphabetic principle that maps the correspondence of spoken sounds and written letters has a profound effect on the way the brain analyses speech and how this feeds into the memory. Such a profound change in our cognitive ability is at the heart of becoming proficient at reading and writing. The task of a primary teacher, therefore, to help children to make this dramatic change is not to be underestimated. This chapter will examine what being 'literate' means and how the four modes of language all interrelate to support this process. It will also review what the challenges are for teachers in helping children become literate. This is made more complex due to the opaque orthography of the English language, so that unlike many other languages letters and sounds do not map directly to each other, and words such as 'enough' are complex to learn to spell and read. Becoming literate in English, therefore, requires mastering the complex alphabetic code.

The challenges faced by teachers are also made more difficult due to the changing curriculum, much of which is driven by political agenda. The impact of these changes and the specific requirements of the current curriculum create constantly shifting demands for teachers. Yet, effective teachers of literacy should base their teaching on research-validated principles that demonstrate their understanding of what works. The chapter will explore what research tells us, including the latest findings from the Education Endowment Foundation on improving literacy. It is hoped that having an understanding of such research will inform practice, as although the National Curriculum states what should be taught, it does not prescribe how it should be done. Understanding what is effective practice is particularly important with many schools becoming academies, enabling them to deviate from the requirements of the National Curriculum. Case studies of different approaches schools have taken help in exemplifying effective practice. A further major consideration for teachers is the increasing number of children who have English as an additional language and the chapter will explore some key factors in teaching English for these children.

What is literacy?

The concept of literacy, Kress argues, is undergoing a revolution, because:

> It is no longer possible to think about literacy in isolation from a vast array of social, technological and economic factors. Kress (2003: 1)

He goes on to explain that two factors have had a particular impact. First, the move away from the written form to the dominance of the image and, second, the move to the screen from the medium of the book. As we are well aware, children are keen users of technology and although social media sites are restricted to children over 13, the media cites many examples of younger children participating (e.g. http://www.telegraph.co.uk/news/health/children/12147629/Children-ignore-age-limits-by-opening-social-media-accounts.html.). It is important to realize that literacy is a cultural social practice and to engage children in reading and writing, we need to link to what they know and what interests them. So if reading on screen is more relevant for a child, then we need to acknowledge this and make use of it. A reluctant reader may not want to read his school reading book, but might well read instructions for his computer game on screen. We need to be conscious that writing has largely moved to be a digital product that often contains innovative layout, images and graphics. Multimodality theory (Kress 2003; Kress and Van Leeuwen 2006) argues that the simultaneous processing of different modes of text, image, sound and gesture in digital texts is a different process from linear sequential reading of print-based text.

The concept of literacy has long been one of intense debate, often called the 'literacy wars' (Coles 2003). This often leads to polarized views on aspects such as phonics versus 'whole language' (Cambourne 2008) and a focus on aspects of language such as grammar and spelling, rather than a focus on composition. Luke and Freebody (1999) have developed a 'four roles' model in considering the concept of literacy. This incorporates (1) breaking the code; (2) participating in understanding the texts; (3) using texts and (4) analysing texts. A learner when engaging in these four adopts different roles. Woolley (2014: 8) notes:

> Rather than treating competencies today in terms of reading, writing, listening and viewing, literacy today is much more concerned with positioning the literacy learner as a participant rather than an inactive recipient of information.

Woolley (2014) cites four factors that impact on literacy:

1 Purpose – learning is valued and meaningful when the purpose of a literacy task is clear.

2 Task – rich learning tasks are purposeful, meaningful and diverse in nature and relate to the role that the learner assumes in completing the task.

3 Text – this refer to what we construct when we speak, listen, read or write. In other words, they can take many forms, including books, videos, blogs, plays and a myriad of other formats.

4 Process/product – refer to the end product or cultural artefact produced in literacy learning. The process concerns social engagement, and products relate to artefacts.

These factors resonate with the case study below that highlights ten factors that can impact on effective literacy teaching.

CASE STUDY: Effective ways to teach literacy

Anna Warren is cited in *The Guardian* (14 February 2013) describing 10 creative ways to teach literacy which echo the aspects cited above. These include:

1 Immersion activities – she says that

> *immersing children in a range of creative activities before reading the text means that they are fully prepared, and excited, about the reading journey ahead of them. Through painting, music composition, a film project, in role drama or sculpture, the children have had a chance to share vocabulary, ideas and concepts which gives their reading fresh meaning and purpose.*

2 Clear Purpose

Anna argues:

> *What's the point of reading and writing anything if you don't know why you're doing it? We aim to provide children with a clear purpose to all reading, and especially writing tasks. Whether it's an invitation to the headteacher to attend a class assembly, an email to an author or an article for a school newspaper, our children know why the quality of their writing matters: because there will be a real audience for their published work.*

3 Professional publishing

She argues that an effective way of valuing children's work is to use a range of ways to publish it. She cites recent examples including:

A whole school bookmaking project. Following a whole school Inset on bookbinding techniques, every class published their own shared book; one example being an anthology of short spooky stories composed by year 6. Their stories were mounted on handmade paper, accompanied with each child's art work (lino cut style prints on metallic paper) with a dramatic paper cut out front cover. The effort the children put into their work was immense, and the results were stunning as a result.

4 Meaningful planning

The school follows the international primary curriculum which provides opportunities to link learning across the curriculum. Staff ensure that they plan meaningful creative activities which ensure that the children will know exactly what they are learning and why.

5 Focused on strategies

There is a focus on teaching strategies particularly for reading. The school ensures that strategies are modelled to children, which could include scanning a text for information, making an inference or creating a mental image. The teachers use 'think aloud' statements for modelling to the children how these skills are used.

6 Inspirational learning environment

The school takes pride in creating an inspirational environment through displaying children's work in creative ways and through providing a range of learning prompts to help the children. Reading corners in classrooms are inviting, well resourced and well organized.

7 Drama to engage and inspire

Led by a drama specialist member or staff, teachers use a range of techniques to explore characters, situations and events.

8 Rigorous teaching of spelling and phonics

Children benefit from tailored teaching of spelling and phonics which is fun, multi-sensory and often physical.

9 Grammar taught creatively

Children understand grammar when they apply it in their writing and when they are encouraged to read with a writer's mind. For example, punctuation rules are drawn from reading shared texts which children have already thoroughly explored.

10 Peer and self-assessment

With clear marking and success criteria and purpose, children mark their own and each other's work. They have seen the teacher's expectations through the teachers' modelling of formative marking. They are well used to looking for learning intentions and checking writing matches any targets and can give constructive feedback.

Pause for thought

1 Consider and discuss where possible with a colleague, how these ten strategies support effective teaching of literacy.

2 In what ways does the school environment support literacy learning?

3 To what extent does the school focus on audience and purpose to support meaningful literacy tasks?

For extensive discussion on creative approaches to teaching literacy, see Chapter 3.

The four modes of language

Teaching English in the primary school requires teachers to consider all four modes of language, that is: speaking, listening, reading and writing. Of these four modes, it is speaking and listening that has been the poor relation and lacked sufficient focus over the years. This is surprising as research, which dates from the Bullock Report (DES 1975) and from the National Oracy Project (Norman 1992), shows that speaking and listening development as well as supporting learning. The term 'oracy' was coined by the National Oracy Project in the late 1980s to provide a more comprehensive term than 'speaking and listening'. To help understand the term 'oracy', Howe (1993) cites four interlinked dimensions that are involved:

1 To enhance learning

2 The ability to use the resource of language (such as vocabulary)

3 The reciprocal social nature of talk

4 The ability to reflect on learning through talk

As a result of the work of the National Oracy Project, in 1988 the National Curriculum gave speaking and listening equal importance to reading and writing in the English curriculum. However, it received a setback when the Primary National Strategy omitted it from its Literacy Framework (1999), which Corden (2000: 4) described as a '*shameful neglect*'. The draft 2014 National Curriculum, in spite of continued research that demonstrated that talk is crucial to learning (Alexander 2000, 2009; Mercer 2000), at first omitted any mention of speaking and listening. However, following a considerable outcry, statutory requirements were included for 'spoken language'. These are not age-differentiated and a single brief programme of study covers the whole of the primary age range, which, again, creates a possibility of undervaluing this key aspect. There is also a danger that the term 'spoken language' used in the 2014 curriculum leads teachers to the misconception that this refers to speaking clearly in Standard English. This would be a narrow interpretation of the need to develop proficiency for talk as the foundation for learning and literacy. Nevertheless, the National Curriculum does state:

> The national curriculum for English reflects the importance of spoken language in pupils' development across the whole curriculum – cognitively, socially and linguistically. (DfE 2013: 14)

Set against this lack of focus on speaking and listening in national curricula and previous strategies, there has been a tendency for schools to put insufficient focus on teaching it, not helped by a lack of depth of understanding by teachers of how to do so effectively. Chapter 3 provides further information on creative approaches that incorporate speaking, listening and drama in the classroom and in Chapter 5 progression in the skills of speaking and listening, and teaching strategies to support these, are explored in depth.

Research study

Deborah Jones (2017) provides a review of oracy in primary education in England. She begins by discussing the terms 'oracy', 'speaking and listening' and 'spoken language'. The term 'oracy' is the ability to understand and use spoken language. 'Speaking and listening' has been criticized for failing to acknowledge the interrelatedness of the two aspects and creating a false dichotomy between the two. 'Spoken language' used in the 2014 National Curriculum is denounced for failing to have the '*connotation of acquired skill that, by analogy with literacy, "oracy" possesses*' (Alexander 2012: 2). Based on a rationale for talk as integral to learning and the significant amount of research which reinforces this, Jones (2017) argues that large-scale projects such as the Languages in the National Curriculum (LINC) (DES 1990) project and the National Oracy Project initially raised the profile of talk and heightened teachers' understanding. Nevertheless, in spite of inclusion in the 1988 National Curriculum of speaking and listening, it was still seen as ambiguous unlike reading and writing. The National Literacy Strategy's lack of mention of speaking and listening in the framework in 1999 was partly remedied by a publication with QCA in 2003 (QCA/DfES 2003) and further guidance published in 2006 (DfES 2006a), but Ofsted reported in its survey of speaking and listening in 2005 that it had not had the attention it deserved and recommended that the use of drama techniques should be extended and speaking and listening taught directly. Although further research has shown the importance of talk for learning (Myhill 2006; Hardman 2011; Littleton and Mercer 2013), it has had limited impact in the classroom. There is a reluctance to engage with this research by teachers, not helped by political views such as those expressed in a statement by the former secretary of state for Education, Michael Gove, who criticized educational theorists who

> have consistently argued for ways of organizing classrooms and classroom activity which reduce the teacher's central role in education. All too often, we've seen an over-emphasis on group work – in practice, children chatting to each other – in the belief that is a more productive way to acquire knowledge than attending to

an expert. (Gove 2013a, https://www.gov.uk/government/speeches/michael-gove-speaks-about-theimportance-of-teaching)

Pause for thought

- How has the changing emphasis on oracy impacted on practice in classrooms?
- Consider why extensive research findings on the importance of talk for learning have had little impact.
- Consider to what extent have political motives had an influence on policy and practice.

Cross-curricular teaching

Definitions of cross-curricular work emphasize that subjects are combined in projects or thematic work, which incorporates a wide range of sources. Arguments for this approach are based on a constructivist view of learning; that is, children learn by direct experience, rather than being told. However, others argue that learning requires clearly delineated boundaries which are provided by single-subject teaching. They argue that an integrated approach is not sufficiently rigorous, especially in teaching fundamental skills. A project cited by the National Teacher Research Panel (2010) found that cross-curricular teaching led to improvement in pupil learning, including questioning, self and group reflection, sharing of ideas and awareness of task requirements. Pupils became more aware of thinking skills and it led to a general rise in confidence in pupils. The case study below cites the impact from one school which used a cross-curricular approach.

CASE STUDY: A cross-curricular approach

Frederick Bird School, in Coventry, is an above-average size primary school with an 82 per cent of pupils from minority ethnic backgrounds who speak English as an additional language. The school won the UKLA Literacy school of the year award for being a school where 'literacy thrives'. Catton (2013), the assistant head for CPD, describes how the school achieved this. The following are important aspects:

- Developing a 'literacy spine', which is a list of quality books that the school has pledged to share with children. Some are read to, and some with, the children and are used in both cross-curricular ways and for literacy lessons.
- Having a literacy toolbox which consists of ensuring classrooms are rich in vocabulary with top tips for writing. Skills for literacy are taught in English lessons, but then applied across the curriculum so that stories, poems, reports and debates can be found in literacy books and the children's theme books covering other areas of the curriculum.
- High-quality professional development for staff is a key factor, which involves experts from outside as well as those from within the school. The school also uses lesson study and peer coaching to support professional development.

Examples of successful projects included the Great Fire of London in Year 2 that covered literacy, science and the humanities, provide powerful examples of supporting children to become independent learners to promote writing and speaking and listening across the curriculum. The children used a website (http://comiclife.com) that allowed them to create diary accounts in the form of comics. They used flip cameras and made news reports of the project. In Year 5 children read *The Messenger Bird* by Ruth Eastham which is a mystery story set in the Second World War and features Bletchley Park and code breaking. The children explored the book through a wide range of speaking and listening and drama activities, leading to creative writing. Children learnt about code breaking in mathematics and made propaganda posters in art. They also constructed mini Anderson shelters. Visits to Bletchley Park and Coventry all helped to bring this project alive for the children. These successful projects illustrate why the school won the UKLA award.

Pause for thought

- In what ways does the school ensure that the environment supports literacy?
- How does cross-curricular opportunities all improve opportunities for developing skills in English?
- In what ways does the school bring projects to life?

Challenges in teaching English

In addition to challenges already discussed such as the changing role of oracy, the English language itself presents challenges for teachers due to what is termed its opaque orthography. This is largely because of the approximate 44 phonemes in English that can be represented in more than 400 different ways. This is unlike many other languages such as Italian, which has only 25 phonemes represented by 24 letters and 8-letter combinations. The irregularities in English are due to the language being derived from several different languages, including Germanic languages, French and Latin. Add to this, the fact that spellings have changed over the years and even those which have remained constant, are often pronounced differently now, it creates particular difficulties in learning to read and write in English. On the surface this would appear to detract from teaching children to read and spell using phonics, however, despite its many contradictions, the English orthography actually has regular spellings for 80–90 per cent of its words (Adams 1990; Crystal 2005). One of the notable features of the patterns contained in the English written language is that the parts of words, known as rimes, contain stable spellings and stable pronunciations. Rimes are parts of words that are spelt the same way, so that in a word such as 'cake' the rime is 'ake' and the initial consonant or consonants are called the onset of the word. Thus, if a child can read or spell 'make', he/she can read and spell 'lake, take, flake, bake, rake', etc. There are 37 rimes in English that provide nearly 500 words (Wylie and Durrell 1970). When such patterns are taught, alongside systematic teaching of all 44 grapheme/phoneme correspondences and the different spelling choices, it is possible to teach children phonics successfully to enable them to decode. Chapter 5 explores the teaching of phonics skills in further detail.

The changing primary English curriculum

As Brundrett and Duncan (2015: 755) note:

> The primary school curriculum in England has undergone multiple, complex and overlapping reforms in the last 20 years (Burton and Brundrett 2005) and a debate on the relative efficacy of a strong emphasis on the basic skills when compared to a broader, more integrative curriculum, has been part of the national debate in the UK for a long time.

The first major milestone in this succession of changes was the introduction of the National Curriculum in 1988, with the next major change being the National Literacy and Numeracy Strategies, which aimed to raise standards and led to a focus on English and mathematics, often to the expense of other areas. Reports by Ofsted in 2009 and 2010 highlighted the problem, and from a survey of 44 highly successful schools, found that creative approaches that made connections across subject boundaries had a positive impact on pupils. At the same time the Rose Review of the Curriculum (Rose 2009) recommended a change from a subject-based curriculum to one that covered six areas of learning, but the UK general election in 2010 and the subsequent change in government, prevented this. At the same time a large research project, the Cambridge Primary Review (2010), led by Robin Alexander, proposed a very different curriculum based on 12 educational aims and 8 domains of knowledge, skill, inquiry and disposition. However, in spite of this research, the coalition government advocated a traditional subject-based curriculum, which was published in 2013. It is clear therefore, that during the period of the last twenty years in England there has been unprecedented change, presenting many challenges for schools.

The key changes in the teaching of English in primary schools in the current curriculum relate principally to the focus on the teaching of spelling, grammar and punctuation (SPAG). One of the main challenges for teachers was the level of knowledge of grammar and the curriculum included about 30 grammar terms, supplemented with a glossary with around another 20 terms. This is assessed in the SPAG test in Year 6 and in 2016 it was introduced also for Year 2 pupils. This presents a significant change from the previous situation in primary schools when grammar was hardly taught (Crystal 2006). As a result, it has required teachers to rapidly improve their own knowledge of grammar. The expectations for trainee teachers have also been revised to ensure a more thorough knowledge of grammar, with the obligatory skills tests for those wishing to undertake initial teacher education course, having been revised in 2012, to include a greater focus on grammar, punctuation and spelling.

A key claim of the new curriculum is, 'Explicit knowledge of grammar ... gives us more conscious control and choice in our language' (DfE 2013: 66). There is evidence (e.g. Myhill et al. 2012) that some types of grammar instruction can improve writing, although as discussed in Chapter 5, a contextualized approach is more successful.

A further key change in the National Curriculum is the emphasis on Standard English and it states, '*Pupils should be taught to control their speaking and writing consciously and to use Standard English*' (DfE 2013: 16).

The Teachers' Standards revised in 2012 (DfE 2011) note that teachers should

> demonstrate an understanding of and take responsibility for promoting high standards of literacy, articulacy and the correct use of standard English, whatever the teacher's specialist subject. (Standard 3, DfE 2011)

This focus on Standard English can present some difficulties for trainee teachers who often worry about their own dialects and accents. In Chapter 8, you will find some guidance on accents, which are the ways in which we pronounce words, and do not relate to Standard English, which can be spoken with any accent. However, sometimes beginner teachers experience difficulties when teaching phonics when their accents differ from the children they teach: think of the pronunciation of *book* and *look*, which in some areas rhyme with *spook*, or the different pronunciations of *grass, path* and *laugh* in different regions. The answer may be to discuss accents with children and, in some cases, to adapt your accent so that the children understand what you are saying. Jolliffe and Waugh (2015: 21) discuss a 'wardrobe of accents', whereby teachers choose one that best fits the situation in which they are teaching, in the same way that we choose clothes to suit the weather.

Dialects involve the words and phrases we use as part of everyday speech, for example different names for bread buns including bap, stottie, barm cake and bun, and different uses of the verb *to be,* such as *we were* (standard) and *we was, we wo*' (non-standard). Standard English is the dialect which is accepted as 'correct' and is what is required when we teach. While we should treasure dialects as part of our cultural heritage, if we do not model Standard English in school and help children to use it when appropriate, we may deny them opportunities to communicate effectively. As Bearne (1998: 4) argues:

> Since standard English is the currency of examination and of literature, media and information texts as well as assumed as part of the writing requirements of most jobs, it is the right of every child to have access to standard forms of language.

Another far-reaching change has been the introduction of the phonics screening check in 2012 for six-year-olds, to monitor the impact on phonics teaching in schools, and reported nationally. This has received considerable debate. The stated purpose of the screening check is to assess whether children have achieved the age-expected level of understanding of phonics and to identify children who may be struggling in developing phonics skills. For those children not achieving the expected level, the aim is to provide additional support, as intervention at an early stage is more effective in helping children to achieve good literacy skills. Objections to the statutory nature of the check include concerns about the resource implications of mandatory testing and the negative consequences when such tests become 'high-stakes' (e.g. Association of Teachers and Lecturers, 2011). Results published by the DfE for 2014 showed that 74 per cent of pupils met the expected standard of phonic decoding, which was an increase from 69 per cent in 2013 and from 58 per cent in 2012. This national assessment has led to an increased focus on phonics and created further pressures for teachers.

Research study: Improving literacy

Education Endowment Foundation (EEF), an independent charity focused on breaking the link between family income and educational achievement, funds evaluations of innovative projects aiming to raise pupils' attainment. One of the most well-known and well-used ways of disseminating this information is through the Teaching and Learning Toolkit (https://educationendowmentfoundation.org.uk/resources/teaching-learning-toolkit). The EEF also produces other resources and more recently it has produced a guidance report on Improving Literacy in Key Stage One and also Key Stage Two. The guidance for Key Stage Two (EEF 2017) cites seven recommendations, based on a range of studies into the teaching of literacy:

1 Develop pupils' language capability to support their reading and writing through purposeful speaking and listening activities.

2 Support pupils to develop fluent reading capabilities which in turn supports comprehension, through guided oral reading instruction and repeated reading.

3 Teaching reading comprehension strategies through modelling and supported practice.

4 Teach writing composition strategies through modelling and supported practice.

5 Develop pupils' transcription and sentence construction skills through extensive practice.

6 Target teaching and support by accurately assessing pupil needs.

7 Use high-quality structured interventions to help pupils who are struggling with their literacy.

(EEF 2017: 1)

Pause for thought

- Consider the importance placed here on speaking and listening to support other modes of language.
- Note how extensive practice is stressed for supporting reading and writing.
- Consider the importance of teacher modelling to help improve literacy skills.

Children who have English as an additional language

In January 2016, there were over a million pupils with English as an Additional Language (EAL) in maintained primary and secondary schools in the UK, a very significant rise from 499,000 in 1997 (DfE 2016a, b; NALDIC 2013). They are certainly not a uniform group: some are new arrivals to the country, some were born here; some are literate in their home language; some are not. NALDIC, in their publication, *The Distinctiveness of EAL*, sum up the task ahead of EAL learners. These children need to learn the English language through the English school curriculum. They also need to socialize with other children and acquire often new social skills, alongside new values, culture and expectations.

To support EAL learners, teachers need to ensure that language teaching needs to be explicit, using correct terms, for example 'Are you going to use an *adjective* or *adverb here*?' Teachers also need to understand pupils' backgrounds and experiences in order to make links to what they know. Three types of EAL-friendly strategies are: substitution tables, which break long strings of language (sentences) into smaller, grammatical, manageable chunks; graphic organizers, which often include an image or diagram to represent a text or concept, and directed activities related to text which are activities which focus pupils' attention on elements of a text. These strategies position language at the forefront, but teach it in a contextualized way. For extensive guidance on teaching English as an additional language, see Trzebiatowski (2017).

Summary

This chapter has been wide-ranging, illustrating the many changes and challenges for teachers in teaching primary English. Use of case studies and research findings illustrate effective ways of dealing with these challenges and many of these aspects are dealt with in further depth in later chapters in this book. One of the key themes has been the importance of speaking and listening, or oracy, to support the development of reading and writing, together with the importance of teacher modelling, practice and intervention for pupils that are struggling.

From reading this chapter you will have developed your knowledge and understanding of:

- conceptions about literacy
- the four modes of language and the importance of speaking and listening
- the challenges of the English language
- cross-curricular approaches to teaching English
- the changing curriculum for English
- research findings into improving literacy
- supporting children who have EAL

Recommended reading

Jones, D. and Hodson, P. eds. (2012). *Unlocking Speaking and Listening*, 2nd ed. London: David Fulton. This provides useful guidance on supporting speaking and listening.

Jolliffe, W. and Waugh, D. with Carss, A. (2015). *Teaching Systematic Synthetic Phonics in Primary Schools*, 2nd edn. London: Learning Matters SAGE.

This supports knowledge about the English language and the teaching of phonics.

Allott, K. and Waugh, D. (2016). *Language and Communication in Primary Schools.* London: Sage.

This book includes a chapter on Language Variation, which may be particularly useful when considering dialect and accent

Trzebiatowski, K. (2017). 'Building Academic Language in Learners of English as an Additional Language: From Theory to Practical Classroom Applications', in W. Jolliffe and D. Waugh (eds.) *NQT: The Beginning Teacher's Guide to Outstanding practice.* (London: Sage, pp. 143–64).

This chapter provides extensive guidance and examples of effective practice in teaching children who have EAL.

Pim, C. (2012). *100 ideas for supporting learners with EAL.* London: Continuum – a good strategies resource for book for teachers of EAL learners.

Chapter 2
Current Developments in Primary English

Chapter objectives

This chapter will help to:

- Explore recent government policy directions and the teaching of English
- Develop an understanding of the concept of 'mastery'
- Understand how 'mastery' can relate to the teaching of English
- Know about current developments in the teaching of English that support 'mastery'
- Have an overview of research findings in the teaching of English related to developing mastery
- Exemplify approaches to mastery through the use of case studies

Introduction

This chapter will focus on current developments in the teaching of English. At a time when the most recent international PISA results in 2016 (http://www.oecd.org/pisa/) demonstrate that East Asian countries, particularly Singapore, are outperforming the UK, the government continues to focus on improving standards. While criticism has been levelled at underlying methodological problems with the PISA study (Prais 2003; Fernandez-Cano 2016), such international tables continue to drive government policy.

Pressure to improve standards in English schools has led to the government focusing on particular methods of developing literacy skills. Most notably this has resulted in an emphasis on the teaching of phonics, and specifically systematic synthetic phonics, which emphasizes the systematic teaching of the grapheme/phoneme correspondences in our language. In addition, the 2014 National Curriculum has placed a heavy emphasis on the teaching of vocabulary, spelling, grammar and punctuation. The National Curriculum Framework document (DfE 2013) provides appendices, which specify progression in teaching these aspects. Chapter 5, which will focus on skills development, will examine teaching of these skills in detail and will emphasize the importance of teaching skills in context.

This chapter will explore the more recent focus on 'mastery' and although this has largely been applied to teaching mathematics, it is receiving increasing attention from schools wishing to improve standards in English. What mastery means for teaching English with examples in practice will be a key part of the chapter. The concept is not without its critics, perhaps because of a lack of understanding of what it means. Didau (2017: 1) calls mastery '*a weasel word which means something different to everyone who uses it*'. Exploring fully what mastery learning means is therefore an important aspect. One implication from the revised National Curriculum is that it should enable greater depth rather than coverage of the curriculum, using strategies such as 'take one book', where a book is studied in depth. Underlying the concept of mastery is the effective use of assessment for learning, and while this has received considerable attention in recent years, principally due to the work of Black and Wiliam (2006; Black et al. 2002; and Wiliam 2011a), there is still a need to ensure that teachers understand and are able to apply this fully to inform their teaching.

What is mastery learning in the teaching of English?

Bit by bit, block by block, we climb our way up a ladder to mastery.

(Joyce et al. 2015: 331)

As Joyce et al. highlight, mastery refers to an approach in which learning is broken down into discrete units and presented in a logical order to enable a deep understanding. It is underpinned by the premise that all pupils can achieve this level of mastery with the right levels of support and that instead of teaching and assessing a specific aspect or subject and then moving on to another one, pupils only move on once they have mastered what has been taught. The concept of mastery is not new and originated in the United States in 1920s (Washburne 1922). In the 1960s Carroll (1963) and Bloom (1968) revived the idea of mastery learning in the form of programmed instruction where learning is divided into small units. Bloom's 'learning for mastery' focused on the underlying philosophy, and his prediction, that 95 per cent of students taught by this method would achieve at a level that had previously only been achieved by 5 per cent of students. In summary there are four concepts involved in mastery learning:

1 It consists of small discrete units of learning.

2 Units are taught in a logical sequence starting with basic components and then moving to more complex ones.

3 There is demonstration of mastery at the end of each lesson, and pupils cannot move on until they have mastered what has been taught.

4 There are additional activities for students needing further practice and extension for others.

Mastery is explained in the final report of the Commission on Assessment without Levels (DfE 2015c: 17), as *'about deep, secure learning for all, with extension of able students* (more things on the same topic) rather than acceleration (rapidly moving on to new content)'. This is a key shift for schools in England from a tendency to focus on coverage of the curriculum and children achieving expected levels in different subjects, to judgements that they are secure in aspects of their learning.

The Education Endowment Foundation (EEF) Teaching and Learning Toolkit provides helpful guidance and evidence about mastery. It explains:

> Mastery learning breaks subject matter and learning content into units with clearly specified objectives which are pursued until they are achieved. Learners work through each block of content in a series of sequential steps. Mastery learning can be contrasted with other approaches which require pupils to move through the curriculum at a pre-determined pace. Teachers seek to avoid unnecessary repetition by regularly assessing knowledge and skills. Those who do not reach the required level are provided with additional tuition, peer support, small group discussions, or homework so that they can reach the expected level.
>
> (https://educationendowmentfoundation.org.uk/resources/teaching-learning-toolkit/ mastery-learning/)

The EEF states that evidence from a number of meta-analyses shows that *'on average, mastery learning approaches are effective, leading to an additional five months' progress over the course of a school year compared to traditional approaches.'* (https://educationendowmentfoundation.org.uk/resources/teaching-learning-toolkit/ mastery-learning/). However, the EEF indicates that the effects are not consistent, which indicates that *'making mastery learning work effectively is challenging'*. The EEF also found that mastery learning is more effective when pupils work in groups or teams. Guskey (1990: 33) found strong links between mastery learning and cooperative learning, which are *'natural complements to each other'*. This chapter will explore this further, in addition to examining first how mastery learning can be applied to teaching English in primary schools, and then discussing recent developments to enable depth rather than breadth of learning across aspects of spoken language, reading and writing.

Mastery and teaching English

Branson and McCaughan (2016) give a possible definition of teaching for mastery related to learning and teaching English as:

> Deeper understanding demonstrated through confident, flexible, independent reading, writing, speaking and listening skills across increasingly challenging contexts.

(https://czone.eastsussex.gov.uk/schoolmanagement/schoolimprovement/
Documents/AWL/AWL%20conference/Teaching%20for%20Mastery%20in%20
English%20Jane%20Branson%20and%20Mark%20McCaughan.pdf)

Mastery in English is also seen as a holistic approach, so that speaking and listening, reading, writing and drama, together with skills such as spelling and punctuation, are integrated, in authentic and meaningful contexts. They are commonly combined through texts, with the emphasis on whole texts being read.

Pause for thought – *Myths about mastery*

There are a number of misunderstandings about mastery. Examine the statements below and decide if they are myths. see page 31 for suggested answers.

1 Mastery does not allow for any differentiation.

2 There is a special curriculum called the 'Mastery Curriculum'.

3 Mastery involves repetitive practice.

4 Mastery learning requires specific textbooks.

5 There is a mastery level that can be achieved in different aspects of English.

Mastery in National Curriculum

The 2014 National Curriculum made a significant change in the principles and methods of assessment, most notably in moving from the assessment of pupils in levels to ensuring all pupils know, apply and understand the matters, skills and processes specified in the relevant programme of study. The report commissioned by the DfE on assessment without levels (DfE 2015c), which followed the introduction of the revised National Curriculum, makes it clear that this curriculum is premised on an understanding of mastery '*which every child can aspire to and every teacher should promote*' (DfE 2015c: 17). The report continues:

> Levels were not consistent with this approach because they encouraged undue pace and progression onto more difficult work while pupils still had gaps in their knowledge or understanding (DfE 2015c: 17).

Chapter 7 will examine assessment in far greater detail; however, it is important to note that changes in methods of assessment have directly led to schools exploring alternative methods and to examining what mastery looks like in different subjects.

In order to investigate this concept more fully, it is useful to review case studies of schools that are using this approach in learning and teaching English.

CASE STUDY: Embedding a mastery teaching approach

One school that has worked at embedding a mastery approach, La Fontaine Academy, describes the process online in the Headteacher Update magazine (see http://www.headteacher-update.com/best-practice-article/embedding-a-mastery-teaching-approach/109277/). The assistant headteacher writes about her approach to setting up a 'Mastery' teaching approach. The aim was to encourage pupils to learn to redraft and improve their own work, and thereby give them a deep understanding of their learning. This began with a series of professional development sessions for staff aimed at explicitly teaching skills that emphasize depth of learning. The school launched this approach by teachers and pupils all doing work based on Austin's butterfly (http://modelsofexcellence.eleducation.org/projects/austins-butterfly-drafts). A short video of this approach can be seen at https://www.youtube.com/watch?v=hqh1MRWZjms. The video shows Ron Berger demonstrating *peer critique* (Berger 2003) (see below). This approach, which involves drafting, focused feedback and response to feedback, was then applied to the teaching of writing in the school. The focus on the use of explicit feedback aimed to support children to make small changes to each draft of a piece of work and improve it each time. To foster this, the school put together 'five steps of feedback' as a guide for how feedback should work in the classroom which included

Step 1: Adult feedback
Step 2: Peer feedback
Step 3: Different adult feedback
Step 4: Different peer feedback
Step 5: Teacher verbal feedback on next step

The process of embedding this took time and constant support; however, it led to the school's results for key stage 1 showing that 91.3 per cent of children were making expected progress or above, compared to a national average of 88 per cent.

Pause for thought

1 Consider why both teachers and pupils worked together to produce drafts here.

2 What are the common difficulties in asking pupils to critique their peers?

3 Why did the school produce a five-step guide to feedback?

Peer Critique

Peer critique, or public critique, is receiving increasing attention from schools. This stems from the work of Ron Berger and his book 'The Ethic of Excellence' (2003), which promotes a culture of craftsmanship in schools and an insistence that if a piece of work isn't perfect it isn't finished. The key part is that pupils need to become accustomed to drafting and redrafting their work. They improve it through public/ peer critique where pupils offer each other advice on how to make it better. Berger gives three principles or rules for getting critique right (2003: 93):

> Be kind. It's essential that the critique environment feel safe, and the class are vigilant to guard against any hurtful comments.
>
> Be specific. No comments as It's good or I like it; these just waste our time.
>
> Be helpful. The goal is to help the individual and the class, not for the critic to be heard.

Berger offers guidelines for critique sessions and also cites two formal critique formats for the classroom:

1 Gallery critique – where the work of every child is displayed and all the work is read. Pupils are then asked to select examples that impress them and reasons for this are discussed. The advantages of this are that every child is encouraged positively to produce a draft, also providing ideas and models of good work and setting a whole-class standard for quality (for examples of gallery critique, and for advice on implementing this approach, see http://www.learningspy. co.uk/assessment/improving-peer-feedback-with-public-critique/).

2 In-depth critique – here the class looks at the work of one pupil, or group of pupils, and spends time critiquing it thoroughly. Advantages of this include teaching the vocabulary and concepts around a specific form and through teaching what comprises good work, it provides modelling of the detailed process of making a piece of work better.

Pause for thought

Look for examples on the internet of teachers using peer critique. You will find one at http://reflectionsofmyteaching.blogspot.co.uk/2013/04/creating-culture-of-critique.html.

Research focus: Lessons of mastery learning

Thomas Guskey (2010) emphasizes that most uses of mastery learning originate from the work of Bloom (1971, 1976, 1984). Bloom proposed that instead of assessment of pupils' progress at the end of a unit of work, checks on progress should be done during the learning and teaching and provide feedback on each pupil's progress. He went on to set out a strategy for teachers in which the learning content is divided into units requiring one to two weeks instructional time and at key points teachers make use of formative assessment that identifies precisely what individual pupils have learnt. This includes targeted suggestions as to what pupils need to do to master the learning. Pupils then undergo further assessments to check their mastery. Bloom believed that most pupils would be capable of learning done in this way. A body of research has confirmed this and shown that pupils in well-taught mastery learning classes achieve better and gain confidence in their ability to learn (Anderson 1994; Guskey and Pigott 1988; Kulik, Kulik and Bangert-Drowns 1990).

Guskey highlights core elements for mastery learning which are required for this to be effective in the classroom. These consist of the following:

1 Diagnostic pre-assessment with pre-teaching: This enables the teacher to assess whether pupils have the prerequisite knowledge and skills for a specific unit or aspect of learning; Studies by Deshler and Schumaker (1993) and Vockell (1993) demonstrate the benefits of relatively brief pre-teaching for pupils where knowledge and skills are shown to be deficient

2 High-quality group-based initial instruction which engages all pupils is at the heart of this approach

3 Progress monitoring through regular formative assessment to systematically monitor pupils' progress

4 High-quality teaching, following formative assessment, to remedy any problems identified: Teachers often use peer tutoring or cooperative learning group work to do this

5 Second parallel formative assessments which follow any reinforcement or additional teaching and offer pupils further opportunities to demonstrate mastery

6 Enrichment or extension activities which are provided to challenge and extend the learning of those pupils who mastered the learning initially and do not require any corrective or additional support

Pause for thought

Consider how you could adopt this mastery learning approach through planning for the following:

- Carefully structuring learning into appropriate units that help build knowledge and skills
- Building in time for formative assessment before a unit of work and pre-teaching where necessary
- Developing further activities to re-teach aspects not mastered
- Developing activities to extend and challenge pupils

Mastery and cooperative learning

Guskey (1990) has emphasized the compatibility of using cooperative learning alongside mastery learning. Cooperative learning involves pupils working together in groups to accomplish shared goals. It differs from 'group work' and requires careful structuring by teachers to ensure that each member of the group makes a contribution to the group's goal. Johnson and Johnson (2000) have identified factors that are essential for cooperative learning to be effective. The most important of these are *positive interdependence* and *individual accountability*. Positive interdependence exists when individuals understand that they cannot succeed unless everyone in the group does and tasks are designed to facilitate this. Linked to this is the necessity for *individual accountability*, where each member of the group must be accountable for his or her share of the work. Other factors that are important include *group and individual reflection* where groups monitor and assess their functioning and ensure the development of the necessary *social and small-group skills* for groups to function successfully.

The use of cooperative learning alongside a mastery approach can be particularly effective in creating a collaborative ethos in the classroom. Pupils work together to support each other using peer tutoring and cooperative group activities. In this way, pupils who have quickly grasped an aspect of learning are able to teach it to their peers and in explaining concepts to others, they extend their own learning. (For further information on implementing this approach see recommended reading, Jolliffe 2007.) Research by Johnson and Johnson (1985), Slavin (1986) and Topping, Duran and Van Keer (2016) reinforces the advantages to all pupils in this way of working. Both cooperative learning and mastery approaches also emphasize the role of the teacher not as the fountain of all knowledge, but instead as the facilitator of learning. As Guskey (1990: 36) comments: '*Students in cooperative learning and mastery learning classrooms thus see themselves and the teacher as a team, on the same side, out to master what is to be learned.*'

Guskey notes that both a mastery learning approach and cooperative learning can be difficult for teachers to implement effectively. However, he points out that when both are used together, they may help resolve many of the difficulties teachers often experience. The difficulties of using a mastery learning approach in a class where there is a wide spread of ability may deter many teachers; however, by creating heterogeneous teams of different abilities and other pupil characteristics, this can provide opportunities for reinforcement and enrichment activities that are motivational, and all pupils are able to gain from peer tutoring and working in teams.

CASE STUDY: Combining cooperative learning and a mastery learning approach

One school in an inner city in the North East of England had been using cooperative learning for some years. This began through using a particular literacy scheme called *Success for All* (http://www.successforall.org.uk/) which incorporates cooperative learning strategies. As a result, in all literacy lessons teachers ensured that pupils worked in teams that were established for around six weeks. A range of cooperative strategies, such as 'reading with your partner', were used where pupils work in pairs to read a page of a book, at their reading level, and their partner listens and asks questions to check understanding, then they swap and the other child reads. Cooperative learning strategies such as talk partners or numbered heads, where each child in a group has a number and a number is called at random to answer a question, all increased engagement by all children. While considerable progress had been seen in attainment of pupils using this literacy scheme, there was still concern that some children were lagging behind. The school therefore decided to incorporate a mastery learning approach.

Following whole-staff training on mastery learning, the English Coordinator and a small team of teachers reviewed English units of work, based on specific texts they would be teaching for the forthcoming term, and then examined how they could incorporate more formative assessment and pre-teaching where necessary. They included additional assessment activities with a key focus on feedback by peers and teachers and provided suggestions for reinforcement and additional challenge to be carried out using peer tutoring and group work. The system of regular tracking of pupils which had already been established was enhanced by breaking this down to smaller levels using a simple APP for ease of recording.

Early indications showed that this combined approach was having an impact by ensuring that teachers were focusing on formative assessment and feedback to a much greater extent.

Pause for thought

1 Consider how both cooperative learning and mastery approaches were complementing each other here.

2 How did the detailed planning of units and opportunities for assessment support this?

3 Why did the focus on formative assessment and feedback appear to be beneficial?

Classroom approaches to mastery learning in English

Schools are experimenting in a number of ways in developing mastery. Some of the particular ways in which this is being done:

1 Building the English curriculum around high-quality whole texts, which the children spend between half and a whole term exploring: The children read the books through shared and individual reading.

2 The teaching of reading, writing and skills in spelling, punctuation and grammar is done in context to help the children understand how to develop as a writer and reader.

3 Extended writing is developed through a number of sessions each week. This is done alongside regular peer critique and feedback.

4 Any child not able to keep up with his or her peers is identified and provided with pre-learning or intervention sessions and, where appropriate, peer tutoring.

5 Focusing on writing, particularly through developing vocabulary, is another approach taken. The 21 Trust in East London has been given funding to work on this aspect (http://www.21trust.org/projects/writing-mastery). The focus is on providing a series of professional development sessions for teachers so that they develop a 'writing toolkit' which includes teaching vocabulary, structuring writing, talk for writing and immersive approaches to writing. This then equips teachers to cascade this knowledge to others in their schools. The programme also enables a professional network of teachers who are committed to improving writing skills in their schools.

6 Another approach to mastery in writing is through shared writing. The concept of modelling excellence echoes the work of Berger (2003:8):

> I believe that work of excellence is transformational. Once a student sees that he or she is capable of excellence, that student is never quite the same. There is a new self-image, a new notion of possibility. There is an appetite for excellence.

Shared writing is not just a demonstration. It is a shared process that should engage pupils through effective questioning and feedback. It helps break down the complex process to enable pupils to achieve mastery. Pie Corbett's work on *Talk for Writing* provides some powerful examples of effective shared writing (see for example the following short video: http://youtu.be/LGMv6Tf-Lm4).

Alex Quigley notes that mastery involves '*the internalising of a pattern of sentence structures and the use of a range of vocabulary and rhetorical devices, until those patterns become automatic*' (http://www. theconfidentteacher.com/2013/03/ shared-writing-modelling-mastery/).

7 In Northern Ireland the curriculum includes a *Thinking Skills and Personal Capabilities* framework for Key Stages 1 and 2 (http://www.nicurriculum.org. uk/curriculum_microsite/TSPC/what_are_tspc/framework/index.asp). This is aimed at focusing on the process of learning rather than the products of learning and at helping pupils develop greater depth of learning. Two specific dimensions are set out (CCEA 2007, Sec 2: 19). First, tasks that range from non-complex to highly complex and second, mastery which progresses from low to high. When high level of mastery with complex tasks is achieved, it demonstrates that a pupil:

> *Shows deep understanding, making connections*
> *Thinks flexibly and creatively, transforming information to create meaning*
> *Thinks critically, questioning and analysing*
> *Sees interrelationships and multiple perspectives*
> *Connects learning spontaneously.*

School approaches that made a difference

There are various examples of schools citing recent innovations that have been successful, following implementation of the revised National Curriculum in 2014, which have been linked to a mastery learning approach. These include:

- Linking topics across areas of the curriculum using high-quality texts.
- Planning longer sequences of work to provide opportunities for children to explore a book in depth for children to discover how writers use language to create desired effects, and then to use these in their own writing.
- Ensuring sufficient time is given to writing and particularly to ensuring that children have opportunities to think and plan their ideas carefully.
- Teaching grammar explicitly and, importantly, in context, as simply knowing and using grammatical features will not necessarily develop good writing.
- Being able to use proofreading, through explicit modelling, to check that writing is effective and accurate.

Pause for thought – *Reflecting on classroom approaches to using mastery learning*

Consider the following questions and where possible discuss with a peer or colleague to deepen your understanding. You will find some suggested answers on page 32:

1 What is the value of using texts to link of aspects of English, and other areas of the curriculum?

2   Why does valuing excellence and modelling it through shared writing support a mastery learning approach?

3   Schools have implemented a mastery learning approach through teachers and pupils working together on aspects, such as writing. Consider why this is effective.

4   In what ways can cooperative paired and group work support a mastery learning approach?

5   Why is assessment for learning and feedback central to a mastery learning approach?

Summary

This chapter has analysed the concept of mastery learning related to English. This is an approach that needs careful implementation for it to be effective. At the heart is the use of effective assessment for learning, centred on the use of feedback. Where schools have developed a comprehensive approach to feedback, including peer critique, this has shown an impact on pupil learning. The revised National Curriculum in England and the significant change from the use of National Curriculum levels for assessment have led to a wide range of innovative and creative practices. In chapter 3 we will explore in greater depth approaches that encourage creativity in order to motivate children to become effective speakers, readers and writers.

Mastery is not the only key priority area at the time of writing. As previously mentioned, the government has continued to focus on skills development, including the central role of phonics in the teaching of reading, and more recently on the explicit teaching of grammar, spelling and punctuation. Chapter 5 will explore these skills in depth; however, as a number of examples cited in this chapter has shown, such skills needs to be contextualized as well as explicitly taught. For some time in learning and teaching phonics the watchword has been 'application', that is in reading and writing. It is only through sufficient opportunities to apply children's learning in phonics, that such learning becomes embedded. This maxim equally applies to grammar, spelling and punctuation.

From reading this chapter you should have a clearer understanding of

- Recent government policy directions for the teaching of English.
- The concept of 'mastery', including recent research findings and how this can relate to the teaching of English.
- A range of ways in which schools have developed mastery learning in the teaching of English.

Recommended reading

DfE (2015). *Final report of the Commission on Assessment without Levels*. London: DFE Publications. This provides the background to the use of mastery learning.

Jolliffe, W. (2007). *Cooperative Learning in the Classroom*. London: Sage. This provides an introduction to cooperative learning and step-by-step implementation.

Wiliam, D. (2011). *Embedded Formative Assessment*. Bloomington, IN: Solution Tree.

This provides comprehensive guidance on how to implement formative assessment and discusses its impact in the classroom.

Answers to pause for thought

1. Myths about mastery

1 Mastery does not allow for any differentiation.

   False: This is a misunderstanding that all children should be doing the same work. What it does mean is that differentiation is not in lesson content, but through a range of strategies such as skilful questioning by the teacher during lessons; identifying and acting on pupil misconceptions; providing challenge for those who have grasped the concept and intervention for those children who are not meeting objectives.

2 There is a special curriculum called the 'Mastery Curriculum'.

   False: A curriculum alone cannot provide a mastery approach. It is an approach and one of the key features is depth of learning rather than breadth.

3 Mastery involves repetitive practice.

   False: This is often cited in relation to mathematics. This misunderstanding is based on the false idea that mastery relates only to mechanical procedures, rather than to concepts. Coupled with the idea that to master a procedure requires repetitive practice at that procedure, this leads some teachers to believe that a mastery approach to mathematics requires repetitive practice with little variation in the items practised for any particular procedure. This is not the case.

4 Mastery learning requires specific textbooks.

   False: The use of any particular textbook does not guarantee a mastery approach. There is also a risk that textbooks can limit expectations and aspirations.

5 There is a mastery level that can be achieved in different aspects of English.

   This is incorrect and the idea of a mastery level which can be assessed is problematic due to the conflict between this idea and the expectation that all children can be provided to full access to the curriculum and can learn what is expected.

2. Reflecting on classroom approaches to using mastery learning

Possible answers include:

1 The value of using texts to link of aspects English, and other areas of the curriculum is principally motivational. It can engage pupils and provide authentic purposes for speaking, listening, reading and writing. It also enables the studying of texts in depth rather than short extracts.

2 Valuing excellence and modelling it through shared writing can support a mastery learning approach as first the teacher is demonstrating what good writing looks like and also the process writers go through, with several attempts or drafts in the process of improving.

3 The main reason why schools have implemented a mastery learning approach through teachers and pupils working together on aspects, such as writing, is that it demonstrates powerfully to pupils that teachers are writers too and that they are endeavouring improving their writing in the same way as pupils. In essence, they become co-learners and the teachers are able to fully understand the process that children are going through.

4 Cooperative paired and group work can support a mastery learning approach, in particular where pupils need further support to fully understand a concept or learn a skill and pupils work together, tutoring each other.

5 Assessment for learning and feedback is central to a mastery learning approach as knowing whether pupils have understood something, or mastered a skill, is vital before moving on to a new aspect and in order to provide support and intervention or extension and challenge activities.

Chapter 3
English as an Irresistible Activity: Promoting Creativity in English

Chapter objectives

This chapter will:

- Clarify what is meant by creativity
- Provide a clear understanding of the features of creativity in the learning and teaching of English
- Review research studies that explore creative approaches
- Show how literature, drama, art, visual texts, film, technology and multimedia can act as a stimulus for creativity
- Review case studies of approaches used in schools

By being flexible, acting spontaneously and responding imaginatively to children's interests and questions, it is argued that creative teachers temper the planned with the lived. (Cremin 2015: 355)

Introduction

This chapter will explore creative approaches to learning and teaching English. It will begin by analysing what creativity means and review examples in practice. A core aspect will be to examine how integrating the four modes of language: speaking, listening, reading and writing through the use of literature, drama, art, visual texts, film and multimedia can support a creative approach. Most of all it will emphasize the importance of children engaging in meaningful, authentic tasks that are relevant and, over which they have ownership: inspiring them to be innovative. In this way, English can become 'irresistible', that is motivating and engaging. Technology can facilitate this, but without teachers who understand the underlying pedagogy no amount of technological equipment, or APPs, can promote creativity. As case studies here will illustrate, schools that are willing to be innovative and redefine learning reap rich rewards. Examining how they do this is at the heart of this chapter.

It is somewhat ironic to note that the last decade in England has shown on the one hand a renewed interest by schools in promoting creativity, and on the other hand, compliance within a climate of extensive accountability, or what Ball calls '*the performativity discourse*' (Ball 1998). But in spite of this, or perhaps because of it, particularly since the publication of *Excellence and Enjoyment* (DfES 2003), schools have explored a range of creative approaches and continue to do so. A project by QCA '*Creativity: Find it Promote it!*' provided materials for schools to engage them in this quest (QCA 2005). At the same time, the establishment of the Creative Partnerships initiative in schools led to links with artists and creative associations to demonstrate how creativity can transform teaching and learning. While funding for the Creative Partnerships project finished in 2010, the focus on creativity continues and creativity is described as one of the four twenty-first-century skills across a number of countries worldwide (http://www.21stcenturyskills.org/). These are skills of critical thinking and problem solving; creativity and innovation and communication and collaboration: or what is termed the 4 Cs: critical thinking, creativity, communication and collaboration. Methods of nurturing these skills in children continue to be the subject of numerous research projects and in June 2016, the EU launched a new skills agenda for Europe (ttps://ec.europa.eu/jrc/en/news/competence-frameworks-european-approach-teach-and-learn-21st-century-skills), aimed at developing these skills.

In England, the revised National Curriculum in England acknowledges the importance of both appreciating creativity and nurturing it, and states that it aims to introduce: '*pupils to the best that has been thought and said; and helps engender an appreciation of human creativity and achievement*' (DfE 2013: 6). In teaching English, and specifically teaching spelling, vocabulary, punctuation and grammar, the National Curriculum makes it clear that '*this is not intended to constrain or restrict teachers' creativity, but simply to provide the structure on which they can construct exciting lessons*' (DfE 2013: 16). How teachers can meet the demands of accountability through inspection and national testing and still 'construct exciting lessons' is a common dilemma. Teaching literacy creatively does not mean neglecting the teaching of skills or essential subject knowledge; instead it refers to using creative contexts that engage children in meaningful activities. This chapter aims to explore this in depth.

Exploring creativity

Although there is a continued focus on creativity worldwide, there is a lack of understanding of the concept. Indeed Barbot et al. note that '*Despite over half a century of systematic research on this topic, this ability is still incompletely understood*' (2015: 371). Craft's work contributed to our understanding and showed that we can be creative in everyday life, differentiating between what she called little 'c' and big 'c' creativity (Craft 2002). The big 'c' type creativity can be associated with achieving major artistic achievements, or what has been called sublime creativity (Cropley 2001), produced by great artists and authors, but this does not mean everyday little 'c' creativity is beyond the reach of everyone. As Cremin et al. (2009: 4) notes that '*creativity involves the capacity to generate, reason with and critically evaluate novel suppositions or imaginary scenarios*'. Schools have found the QCA framework helpful in broadening understanding of what is involved in creative learning and teaching, including

- Questioning and challenging
- Making connections and seeing relationships
- Envisaging what might be
- Exploring ideas, keeping options open
- Reflecting critically on ideas, actions and outcomes

(QCA 2005: 10)

In 2007 the National College for School Leadership (NCSL) highlighted that creativity is not a '*bolt on to the curriculum*', but instead '*central to the whole process*' (p. 4). Examples of creativity at the centre of the curriculum will be explored in this chapter.

Pause for thought – *What is creativity in English?*

From reading the previous section, examine the English activities below and decide to what extent they show a creative approach to learning and teaching. There are no right or wrong answers; it is more appropriate to consider the degree to which they are creative.

1   In Reception, the children had been reading 'Handa's Surprise' by Eileen Brown. They had read the story and enjoyed an animated version. They then explored the story in the role-play area, which was decorated with scenes from Africa, showing different animals. There was a short video playing, showing a 'travel guide to Kenya'. They used story masks of animals and props including a selection of fruit, dressing up clothes and baskets. This led to creating their own adaptation of the story which they explored orally, and in shared writing the class produced a printed version illustrated by the children. Finally the children acted out their story in the class assembly.

2   A Year 3 class was learning about speech marks in punctuation. They explored these using sticky notes denoting speech bubbles. Working in groups they researched pictures of famous characters from books, chose their favourites and together decided on typical things these characters would have said, such as Captain Hook from Peter Pan saying 'Now you'll walk the plank' and 'Listen to the sound of the clock ticking. The crocodile is coming for you!' They rehearsed these in role and then wrote the dialogue on sticky notes which

were stuck to the pictures and displayed. The groups then swapped pictures and then, working in pairs, had to write a short character portrait, including what the character said, to show correct punctuation.

3 A Year 4 class were studying the Tudors in history and the teacher decided to link activities in English to this topic. Pupils wrote fictional accounts of the great fire of London as well as producing paintings of this event.

4 In Year 6 the children had been reading spooky stories. They looked at examples in pairs to decide how these effects were achieved. They improvised in drama some scenarios with atmospheric music; explored pictures of spooky scenes and then created a corner of the classroom using a range of props, as a haunted house. The class went on to create an anthology of spooky stories. Using iBooks software, they published their own book, containing illustrations, sound effects and short video clips that they had filmed themselves.

Research study: Making English 'irresistible': Relevance, control, ownership and innovation

Jeffrey's (2006) ethnographic study of creative features found in a sample of schools illustrated four key aspects that characterize creative teaching and learning: relevance, control, ownership and innovation. The schools and colleges in the sample all used the same structure in their projects consisting of a critical event to initiate the process, with involvement from outside advisers and artists and a creative use of space, within and outside the classroom. They adjusted normal boundaries of time beyond the usual lesson length such as weeks set aside for specific curriculum investigations, time for presentations and regular celebrations. They also went through well-defined stages of conceptualization, preparation and planning, divergence, convergence, consolidation and celebration, and all involved 'open adventures' (Jeffrey, 2006:10). The study demonstrated:

> The young participants engaged meaningfully with learning when they had an opportunity to own the knowledge they encountered or the processes with which they were engaged. (2006: 13)

The four recurrent aspects that were found in each school are detailed further below.

Relevance

Relevance refers to learning that is meaningful to the immediate needs and interests of pupils. Pupils in the study were able to bring their own experiences and imagination to the learning situations. Due to the nature of the activities, pupils were often able to engage in different ways. They were able to draw on a range of abilities, or what Gardner (1983) has called 'multi-intelligences'. The activities also altered the teaching relationships as the pupils acted as both teacher and learner through engaging in small groups and undertaking investigations.

Control

In the schools sampled, pupils were self-motivated and not governed by extrinsic factors, or task set solely by the teacher. They became authors of their own learning and saw their efforts as worthwhile or as Jeffrey says: '*The learners engaged in taking off and taking over*' (2006: 11).

Ownership

In each school, pupils learnt for themselves – not for the teacher's, or anyone else. Creative learning in this way was internalized and made a difference to pupils. It also engendered a social identity and a sense of belonging. Jeffrey (2006: 13) notes:

> These situations provided assurances for the young participants that manifestations of their 'selves' as individual and unique learners were valued and safe because personal perspectives and what might, at times, be seen as idiosyncrasies were acceptable and contributed to the general dynamic culture. In this way they felt able to be creative and innovative.

Innovation

These critical events and the stages they went through encouraged pupils to be curious and take risks and act spontaneously. In this way they were innovative, so that

> something new is created. A major change has taken place – a new skill mastered, new insight gained, new understanding realized, new, meaningful knowledge acquired. A radical shift is indicated, as opposed to more gradual, cumulative learning, with which it is complementary. (Jeffrey 2016: 4)

These four factors of relevance, control, ownership and innovation can act as invaluable guidelines in generating creative learning activities. To help you reflect on this study, the following table examines this process further.

Pause for thought

Considering the four key aspects of relevance, control, ownership and innovation, develop some appropriate questions to aid the planning of creative activities in English. A few examples have been provided. You will find some suggested answers on page 50.

Stage	Relevance	Control	Ownership	Innovation
Conceptualization and planning	How relevant is the proposed project to the lives of the children?		What flexibility will be allowed?	What will be new in the process or final product?
Exploration – divergence and convergence	How will the children review and revise their work?			
Consolidation – final product/process		Will children decide on the final product?		
Celebration				Can the project be celebrated in innovative ways?

How can teachers promote creativity?

In order to explore the development of creative projects, guidelines from QCA (2005) are helpful in planning these in the classroom:

1 Set a clear purpose for pupils' work – this is very much about how units of work are structured which take pupils through the process step by step and consider allowing sufficient time so that too much is not planned for one lesson.

2 Be clear about freedom and constraints. It is important to allow pupils choice in ways of working and to shape the direction of work, but at the same time providing clear time scales or resources which can stimulate improvisation and response.

3 Fire pupils' imagination through different ways of learning and experiences. This could be through a range of stimulus including visitors and artists or problems or real-world events, making sure the experiences are relevant to pupils' lives and build on what they find interesting or experience in their lives.

4   Give pupils opportunities to work together ensuring that collaborative work is carefully managed and monitored.

5   Establish the criteria for success and help pupils to judge their own success and to appreciate and critique the work of their peers.

6   Capitalize on unexpected learning opportunities through making the most of unexpected events, sometimes putting aside the lesson plan and 'going with the moment' if it is felt this will be effective for pupils' learning.

7   Ask open-ended questions and encourage critical reflection using questions such as: 'What if?' 'Why is?' and 'How might you?' to encourage pupils to see from different perspectives.

8   Regularly review work in progress and particularly help pupils to give and receive constructive feedback.

Research Focus: Creative arts and literacy

A project by the Centre for Literacy in Primary Education (CLPE) (CLPE 2005) worked with a group of nursery and primary school teachers and children together with 'arts partners' from the fields of drama, storytelling, visual arts, film-making, multimedia, dance and performing arts. The CLPE aimed to investigate how children's work in creative arts influenced their literacy development. As they state (2005: 199):

> There is no quick or simple transition from creative arts to literacy, but the creative arts, because they are fundamental ways of symbolising meaning, provide a powerful context for developing language and literacy.

The results showed a 'stunning variety of talk' (2005: 117) among children, and between children and adults, demonstrating increased confidence in speaking and listening. This array of talk led to generating ideas for writing, and children were observed writing spontaneously and enthusiastically after engaging in storytelling, drama, music or artwork. This was principally due to having actually experienced something and having a context for their writing. They wrote in different forms using storyboards, scripts or drawings with words which all encouraged children to engage in the process.

Pause for thought – *Reflections on research study*

The CLPE study cited above provides many rich examples of children's projects that are worth exploring (see https://www.clpe.org.uk/sites/default/files/Many%20 routes%20to%20meaning%20childrens%20language%20and%20literacy%20 learning%20in%20creative%20arts%20work_0.pdf).

In reflecting on this consider

- What were the benefits from working in this way?
- In what way can such projects be replicated in other classrooms?
- What are the potential barriers and how could these be overcome?

Classroom approaches to learning and teaching English creatively

The power of play

As the foregoing research study showed, the use of the creative arts can be a powerful stimulus for literacy. Another factor that can also support this includes considering how elements of play can be fostered. Too often play is seen as the domain of early years classrooms and yet being given the chance to explore playfully, either using role-play, or within a particular context created in the classroom (such as a travel agents), it can support all the key elements of relevance, control, ownership and innovation. This is largely because it taps into children's imagination. It was Vygotsky who highlighted that imagination is the engine of children's creativity. Written in 1930 and re-published in 2004, he acknowledged:

> We can identify creative processes in children at the very earliest ages, especially in their play. A child who sits astride a stick and pretends to be riding a horse; a little girl who plays with a doll and imagines she is its mother; a boy who in his games becomes a pirate, a soldier, or a sailor, all these children at play represent examples of the most authentic, truest creativity. ([1930] 2004: 11)

He also argued that ([1931] 1991) imagination and thinking play a vital role as they combine to help children understand the world that surrounds them.

Craft (2002) argues that possibility thinking is at the heart of all creativity in the early years. She proposes that this is the means by which questions are posed or puzzles surface. One example of playful activities, cited by Cremin et al. (2009), is of a class of 6–7 year-olds where a range of creative activities were triggered by reading the 'Little Wolf's Book of Badness' by Ian Whybrow. The teacher used different examples of books about wolves to challenge children's thinking about 'big bad wolves' and then explored Little Wolf's adventures. (An animated version can be seen at https://vimeo.com/75795102.) The book is written in the form of letters from Little Wolf sent to his parents. Little Wolf chronicles his sluggish journey to *Uncle Bigbad's Cunning College for Brute Beasts* where he is sent to learn the 'nine rules of badness'. Work on the book involved turning the classroom role-play area into 'Beatshire' and the 'Frettnin Forest' and supported much imaginative play. This led to a range of literacy activities and activities including developing 'rules of badness' and support for Little Wolf's spelling problems. A number of children also wrote letters in the style of Little Wolf which demonstrated their engagement through writing in role.

Play does not have to be restricted to the early years. One of the most powerful examples of engagement in literacy witnessed by the author involved a type of role-play in a Year 10 classroom during the teaching of an English lesson. The pupils had to work in groups to come up with a clear plan for a school prom and to consider venue, cost, type of music, dress, etc. The project was divided into stages over a series of lessons, starting with an oral report, developing costed projects which were presented in a choice of formats, and, following voting for the preferred proposals, ending in a Dragon's Den type pitch to the headteacher with accompanying written proposals. Pupils were keenly engaged in this project and it demonstrated a meaningful context, real ownership and an authentic audience for their finished work.

Talk as a key component

A key component in creative activity in the classroom is the use of talk for learning.

Britton famously wrote: '*Reading and writing float on a sea of talk*' (1970: 164).

The work of Pie Corbett on 'talk for writing' has demonstrated the potential of improving writing following opportunities to explore a text through talk. Talk for writing (http://www.talk4writing.co.uk) uses a staged process of oral rehearsal before writing. The process involves three key stages: first, imitation where the children become fully familiar with the text, and its language patterns and structure, through a range of oral activities. The second stage is innovation of the text type where elements are developed, extended or altered. This involves shared writing where the children and teacher co-construct a text. Finally, they invent their own stories in the same genre, and in independent application, children refine and revise their work. Talk is embedded in every stage of the writing process. Full details can be found at http://webarchive.nationalarchives.gov.uk/20130401151715/ https://www.education.gov.uk/ publications/eOrderingDownload/DCSF-00467-2008.pdf

One of the core elements of Talk for Writing is the use of storytelling. Telling a story is a powerful way to engage children, and from the author's own experience of this, it can really enhance children's listening and their ability to recall. The rapt look of over 200 children's faces in a school assembly as they listen to a story being told, so that you can literally 'hear a pin drop', has to be experienced. When stories in a sequence are told, the fascinating aspect is that the children often remember the details of previous stories better than the storyteller! As Grainger (1997: 10) highlights:

The oral tradition of storytelling underpins and complements the growth of language and literacy. Its spellbinding power can liberate children's imaginations, release their creativity and enable them to weave dreams together, as they journey along the road of never-ending stories.

For teachers to gain the skills to become proficient storytellers, the following are useful steps:

- Begin with a personal tale, a memorable moment, perhaps accompanied by a photograph or object.
- Try a well-known traditional tale – such as the *Three Little Pigs* in order to build confidence and use props such puppets, or a storysack.
- Internalize the story – use story maps or story summaries. It is necessary to write or draw these yourself, as it is the process that helps internalize the story. It is important to realize that no retelling of a story will ever be the same, as in the telling certain adaptations and embellishments will naturally occur.
- Practise to develop confidence, particularly your use of voice so that expression, tone, range and volume vary appropriately.
- Observe a professional storyteller to gain an insight into some of the ways they engage an audience, such as typical storytelling openings which instantly set the scene:
  - Not in your time, not in my time, but in the old time, when the earth and the sea were new …
  - Once there was and once there was not …
  - Snip, snap, chin, my story's in.

As well as the use of props, a storytelling chair can be useful in the classroom. One of the important aspects is that after modelling by the teacher of storytelling, to encourage children to engage in this. Providing story boxes with props, particularly if they are linked to a story the children have been told, can be helpful for young children. For older children, working in pairs to tell anecdotes, stories and jokes can be helpful.

As the next section will explore, storytelling can link to a range of drama activities, which are all powerful in developing skills of speaking, listening, reading and writing.

Drama as a tool for creativity

Drama is a powerful tool for engaging children in learning and inspiring creativity. It is particularly useful in analysing a text, leading to a range of writing. Exploring a dilemma in a story through improvisation, for example, can be an effective stimulus for writing. Cremin et al. (2006: 15) cites a research study, connecting drama and writing, which found:

> During their engagement in tense dramatic encounters the children in this research project were brought to the brink of writing and on these occasions their writing seemed to flow from the imagined context with relative ease.

Drama can range from the informal playground games to more formal theatre-type performances. The use of drama techniques that can be incorporated into many lessons can spark creativity and do not require large spaces such as a school hall. Types of drama techniques or conventions that are useful include:

- *Teacher in role* – the teacher becomes the character in a story or improvisation. It can help model the language and actions of a character. The use of a prop such as a hat or cloak to denote the teacher is in role is useful in signalling this to the class.

- *Decision alley or conscience alley* – the class create two lines facing each other. One child in role as a particular character walks down the 'alley' between the lines. The class voice the character's thoughts, both for and against a particular decision or action which the character is facing, acting as his or her conscience.

- *Freeze frame* – involves children selecting a key moment, and creating a still picture to illustrate it.

- *Thought tracking* – using a freeze frame moment involves the rest of the class in contributing ideas as if they were speaking the thoughts of one of the characters. These can support or contrast with the words that the characters actually say. The class can make a circle around the character and say their thoughts one at a time, or individual children can stand next to the frozen character and speak their 'thoughts' aloud.

- *Hot seating* – puts one person in role, often as a character from a book or play, usually seated and facing the class. Others ask questions, and the response should be consistent with the role.

- *Mime* – children work with actions rather than words to convey elements of a character or their emotions.

Storyline

Storyline is an approach that combines narrative, drama, art and other areas of the curriculum. It engages children in collaborative investigations and incorporates multimedia. Over a period of four to six weeks a fictional world is created in the classroom. Working in small groups, learners take on the roles of characters in a story and keep these roles throughout the Storyline topic. The story, set in a specific place and time, has a clear beginning, middle and end, usually concluding with some kind of celebration. The narrative unfolds as the learners work together on key questions. These open questions, based on curriculum content, structure and provide narrative impetus for the story in the same way as chapters in a book. For instance, the key question 'Who are you?' often starts the Storyline by establishing the people. The learners in agreement with their group create a character individually; making a stick puppet, papier maché doll, or a drawing, to represent the character, then they write about the character, and introduce themselves in role as a group to the rest of the class. A later question, heralding a development in the story, might be introduced following the receipt of a letter or the arrival of a 'visitor' (such as a class teacher or a colleague), asking for help. Key questions are a vital component in the Storyline approach as they incorporate subject content into the story in a meaningful way and thus motivate the learners to engage with it. For more guidance on setting up a Storyline project, see Ahlquist (2013) and http://www.storyline-scotland.com/. Review the case study below to see a storyline project in action.

CASE STUDY: Storyline and Ancient Egypt

In this example, a Year 3 class in Scotland arrived in school one morning to find a large poster showing a picture of Tutankhamen with a sign underneath saying:

> 'Lady Mancini needs YOU for a archaeological expedition to Egypt!' It stated that those who were 'fit and healthy, willing to work in a team, prepared to live in the heat and ready to research and report' were asked to apply for a place on the expedition. The teacher had a personal contact in Egypt so actual correspondence took place between the person taking on the role of Lady Mancini, the archaeologist, and the children in the class.

Lady Mancini enjoyed her role and she became the lynchpin of the project. The children wrote to her, emailed her and made characters for her. She set them challenges along the way. She told the children about a school she visits in Cairo and the plight of the children who attend. She also sent photos of herself on an 'archaeological dig'. (Her neighbours had builders in and had left a pile of sand in the garden.) Other photos included Lady Mancini walking down a pyramid shaft holding a candle to light her way – (she was in the small corridor heading to her utility room!) When the children heard she was coming over to visit them they were delighted. The children had been working in groups of character experts, for example, fashion designers, archaeologists for pyramids, archaeologists for mummies, theologians, linguists and historians. They decided to prepare presentations of their learning for Lady Mancini's visit. This culminated in a highly successful event.

The teacher reflected that:

> Taking part in a Storyline topic allows for the development of the four capacities specified in the Scottish Curriculum for Excellence: effective contributors, successful learners, confident individuals and responsible citizens. The Storyline approach allowed children to connect with their learning in a deep and meaningful way. Through role-play, in which they become the characters in the story, pupils actively engaged with the Storyline.

(For further details, see http://www.storyline-scotland.com/wp-content/uploads/2012/05/egypt.pdf)

Pause for thought

- What was effective in encouraging the children to engage in this project?
- How did working in role support this?
- How effective was having a genuine audience for the children's work?

Visual texts as a stimulus

The use of pictures can also act as a stimulus for creative work. The rich potential of picture books to trigger children's 'possibility thinking' (Craft 2002) is worth exploring. While picture books are commonly used with young children, the many excellent examples of picture books for older children can also encourage divergent and critical thinking. For excellent examples, see 'The Highwayman' by Charles Keeping, or 'Beowulf' by Michael Morpurgo and also the work of Anthony Browne, for example 'Changes', or 'The Tunnel', to help explore a number of dilemmas and issues.

Pantaeleo's (2015) study of the impact of pupils learning to read and create images based on the study of the visual elements of art and design in picture books and graphic novels found that a multimodality approach acknowledges the contribution of different modes, such as speech, writing, image, music, gesture, gaze, and posture, to communicate meaning. As teacher and researcher she noted the impact:

> Students' understanding of the meaning potential or the affordances of various semiotic resources of image will affect their examination, comprehension, appreciation, analysis, interpretation and design of both print and digital multimodal texts. (2015: 126)

CASE STUDY: *The Promise*

Using *The Promise* by Nicola Davis, which describes the journey of a young girl from a pickpocket to an environmentalist, and exemplifies the interrelationship between the words and pictures, Hendy (2016) provides a vivid example of the impact of using this book in the classroom. Using the powerful images in the book as a stimulus for a choice of drama activities (for an animation, see https://vimeo.com/73026206), children then chose from of a range of writing, including

- A description of the young thief and her life
- Dialogue (to include action and characterization)
- A short story inspired by *The Promise*
- A postcard to the author, Nicola Davies, detailing children's personal responses to the text

Completed stories were sent to the author, which resulted in not only a response thanking them, but also sharing a draft of a book due to be published a few weeks later. This demonstrated not only the power of such picture books, but also the importance of a real audience and purpose for writing.

> **Pause for thought**
>
> - How did this picture book stimulate such a range of responses?
> - How important was choice in the drama and writing activities?
> - What was the impact of providing a real audience for the children's stories?

Take one picture

Take one picture, is the National Gallery's countrywide scheme for primary schools. (http://www.takeonepicture.org.uk/picture/index.html). The Gallery focuses on one painting each year to inspire cross-curricular work in primary schools. It begins with a one-day professional development course for teachers. Schools are then challenged to use the image imaginatively in the classroom both as a stimulus for artwork, and for work in more unexpected curriculum areas. A range of the products of this work are displayed on the National Gallery's website which include creative writing, collage, sculpture and print-making.

Hertfordshire Grid for Learning has developed this concept into 'Take one book' where a book is explored in depth and writing in a range of genres follows. See https://www.hertsforlearning.co.uk/sites/default/files/user_uploads/00_news/documents/english_nate/nate_te_primary_matters_michelle_nicholson_2.pdf for further details.

Film

Film is another powerful stimulus for a range of literacy activities. The British Film Institute (BFI) has driven this work in schools and provided a range of resources for use to support the effective use of film. Its teaching guide *Look Again!* (BFI 2003) is available online (http://www.bfi.org.uk/sites/bfi.org.uk/files/downloads/bfi-education-look-again-teaching-guide-to-film-and-tv-2013-03.pdf). The BFI has also produced further guidance 'Using Film in Schools' (BFI 2010) which provides useful tips on creating films; practical advice on equipment and a review of opportunities for using film across the curriculum. Suitable short film clips can be obtained from http://shop.bfi.org.uk/education-resources/. The Literacy Shed website also provides links to a number of excellent examples: http://www.literacyshed.com/. You can also find a large number of suitable clips on YouTube.

Ofsted (2010) cite a range of creative approaches in schools that have been shown to raise standards, including the use of film. The following case study cited by Ofsted showed how beginning with a film, activities helped one Year 2 class to be more analytical, collaborative and imaginative.

A Year 2 teacher combined reading and writing with other approaches to interpretation, evaluation and presentation. He encouraged pupils to make connections, ask questions and reflect critically on ideas and actions. He had chosen a Japanese film, My Neighbour Totoro, as the stimulus for learning, splitting the film into sections to study different aspects of the story. This session came as the culmination of work with pupils through which they had learnt to analyse film from the different standpoints of setting, sound, action and language. Discussion at the start of the session demonstrated that the pupils had a good understanding of these categories.

Each pupil was given a small whiteboard with the different categories as headings. During the first showing of the film clip, the teacher helped pupils identify key moments for focusing on the areas for analysis. During the second showing, pupils used the whiteboards to record their own responses across any categories they chose. They discussed their observations and evaluations, showing considerable knowledge and an ability to challenge each other constructively. They not only questioned and challenged each other's responses to the clip 'as film'; they showed curiosity and imagination in exploring the culture and assumptions that had shaped the film.

Finally, each pupil wrote an ending for the story they had been watching.

The writing was highly imaginative, with a strong sense of place and, in many cases, a sophisticated vocabulary and range of expression.

(Ofsted 2010: 27–8)

Technology

Technology, carefully planned, can be a further means to stimulate and support creative learning and teaching in English. Andrews (n.d.) describes a unit of work on Lewis Carroll's *Alice in Wonderland* and how the use of APPs helped to create engagement in the text and enabled the children to create their own innovative versions. The work went through phases, starting with becoming fully immersed in the text, then examining the features of the text, before going on to create new versions. They also made links to other texts that explored similar themes such as the *Narnia* stories by C. S. Lewis, *The Tunnel* by Anthony Browne and the film *Instructions* by Neil Gaiman (see https://www.youtube.com/watch?v=Ra4pZ3OTUKA).

APPs were used to enhance the engagement and the final products. These included *Tellagami*, an APP which enables an avatar to be created, a setting, and including writing suitable things for the avatar to say. Another useful APP is Socrative which has one version for the teacher, 'Socrative Teacher', and one for the children 'Socrative student'. This enables the teacher to ask a range of questions and the children to respond on their iPads. The advantage being that the teacher can see all the children's contributions instantly. Following examining how the author had created particular effects, the children went on to imitate and produce their own original work. Here the APP *Corkulous* was used to help the planning process. This APP is essentially an ever-expanding cork board, which acts as a working wall on which children can collect images, film clips, ideas, sentences, etc., to be organized and used later in their writing. The next phase was to 'try it out' and the children practised the authorial skills they learnt and applied themselves in writing. In the final publication stage, the APPs Book Creator and also Puppet Pals were used. Book Creator enables publishing writing in an e-book which can then be stored in an iTunes library. Puppet Pals enables a recording of a narrative and to physically move the characters around the set.

Andrews notes about this project:

> Children's writing no longer needs to be published in their English books. Whether they are published digitally, in a beautiful class anthology, on tea-stained paper or kept in the pirates' chest, it is often enough to spur the children on to produce their best writing. With the world of multi-media, I believe we have the ideal medium to entice the reluctant writer into producing his or her own masterpiece. (p. 17)

This project demonstrates the use of technology to support the learning and it is important to ensure that APPs and other software or types of devices do not drive the learning, but instead aid it.

CASE STUDY: Immersive social learning

One academy based in Lincoln, Hartsholme Academy, has developed a particularly innovative approach to learning which they describe as immersive and experimental.

One of the other key aspects is that children design their own learning area. They are also presented with challenges and a range of resources to stimulate them. Children work collaboratively, usually without tables and chairs, and are encouraged to use both the indoor and outdoor classroom. Headteacher, Carl Jarvis, describes this vision of social learning in a presentation available as a TEDX talk and available on https://www.youtube.com/watch?v=2uigDjZkoWY. He explains that this begins with the interests of the children and is designed to stimulate and connect the learning across the curriculum in social ways. This approach centres around

- Designing learning environments that are relevant and engaging
- Designing environments that stimulate and connect the learning
- An understanding of how 'children tick'.

One example of a typical project took place in Year 6. The class was looking at moments in history. In a blacked-out classroom that was decorated as a Medical Centre, with desks transformed into hospital beds, they were delving into the 9/11 disaster. Large screens replayed news footage as that afternoon in September unravelled and there was almost an eerie atmosphere in the room. Pupils were imagining they were in Lower Manhattan and were writing reports on the events. One group of pupils used chalk to detail the happenings on the floor, while his peers typed their reports on their iPads or videoed each other's verbal reports.

Each term the curriculum is designed around one questions, for example, 'Can we create a food revolution?' In one Year 2 class, the classroom was designed as a farm with straw bales in the centre of the classroom (see https://www.youtube. com/watch?v=e6neUgB9l-g).

One of the key observations made when visiting this school is the level of engagement of the pupils. In one Year 5 class, the teacher announced it was playtime and the children could leave their work and go out to play, or continue if they wished to. To the amazement of visitors to the school, not one child decided to go out to play. Work was play. The results of this creative curriculum and approach to learning has led this school to improve from being deemed by Ofsted to be in Special Measures, to being outstanding within two years and the school is now achieving consistently within the top 5 per cent of all schools.

Pause for thought

- Why has this approach to learning been so successful?
- How does the environment stimulate learning?
- How does this case study illustrate learning that is relevant, over which children have control and ownership and helps innovation?

Summary

This chapter has discussed what is meant by creativity and illustrated this through a range of case studies and research projects. It has demonstrated the need to connect learning and as Bearne, Grainger and Wolstencroft (2004) note, working in multimodal ways we can redefine what we mean by 'literacy'. Using literature, storytelling, visual texts, art, music, drama, film and technology, we can stimulate children to learn and develop speaking, listening, reading and writing. The four key aspects to support this process, as this chapter has shown include relevance, control, ownership and innovation. These emphasize the importance of children engaging in meaningful, authentic tasks that are relevant and, over which they have ownership: inspiring them to be innovative. In this way, English can become 'irresistible', that is motivating and engaging.

In this chapter you will have developed your knowledge and understanding of

- The meaning of creativity
- Features of creativity in learning and teaching English
- Research studies that explore creative approaches
- How literature, drama, art, visual texts, film, and technology and multimedia can act as a stimulus for creativity
- A number of approaches used in schools

Recommended reading

British Film Institute (BfI) (2003). *Look Again!* Available at http://www.bfi.org.uk/education/teaching/lookagain/

Provides useful guidance on using film in the classroom and also:

British Film Institute (BfI) (2010). *Using Film in Schools*. Available at http://www.bfi.org.uk/education-research/education/education-resources

Copping, A. (2016). Being Creative in Primary English. London: Sage

Cremin, T., Bearne, E., Dombey, H. and Lewis, M. (2009). *Teaching English creatively*. London: Routledge.

This book provides comprehensive guidance to different aspects of teaching English creatively.

Waugh, D. and Jolliffe, W. (2017). *English 5-11: A guide for teachers*. Abingdon: Routledge. Chapter 3 discusses a range of creative approaches to teaching literacy.

Suggested answers to pause for thought

Planning a creative project – possible responses

Stage	Relevance	Control	Ownership	Innovation
Conceptualization and planning	How relevant is the proposed project to the lives of the children?	How will the children take control?	What flexibility will be allowed?	What will be new in the process or final product?
Exploration – divergence and convergence	How will the children review and revise their work?	Will the children decide on different routes they take during the project?	Will children be able to decide on the types of end products or writing they produce?	How will innovation be encouraged?
Consolidation – final product/ process	Will the final product or process be relevant to the children's lives or experiences?	Will children decide on the final product?	How will the children demonstrate their own initiative?	Will there be choice over the final product/ process?
Celebration	Will the product be celebrated in ways that show it is valued?	Will children be able to decide on the type of celebration?	Will the celebration be planned and implemented by the children?	Can the project be celebrated in innovative ways?

Chapter 4
English as a Practical Activity: Being a Reader

Learning objectives for this chapter

By reading this chapter you will develop your understanding of the following:

- What it means to be a reader and how teachers can develop both their pupils' and their own reading skills and understanding
- The key role that teachers play, not only in teaching the basic skills of reading, but also in motivating children to become real readers who view reading as a valuable life skill and a source of pleasure
- Ways of making reading an attractive and engaging activity for children
- The importance of engaging children with poetry as well as stories, digital texts and non-fiction

Introduction

The overwhelming majority of children in England leaves primary school able to read competently, but many might not be described as readers, in the sense that they rarely read for pleasure (PIRLS 2011). In 2014, 89 per cent of Year 6 children achieved the expected standard for reading (Level 4) in SATs tests in England, with 50 per cent achieving level 5 or above. Since then the expected standard and the tests have changed and levels are no longer used, so the fact that only 66 per cent achieved the expected level in 2016 should not be taken as evidence of a decline (DfE 2016a, b).

In international studies, such as PIRLS, England compares well with other countries. For example, in 2011 only five out of the 45 countries involved, Hong Kong, the Russian Federation, Singapore, Finland and Northern Ireland, performed significantly better than England. However, there was a wider spread of attainment in England than in the other high-performing countries (Higgins 2013).

Figure 4.1 Attainment at key stage 2 reading between 1997 and 2014 (DfE 2015)

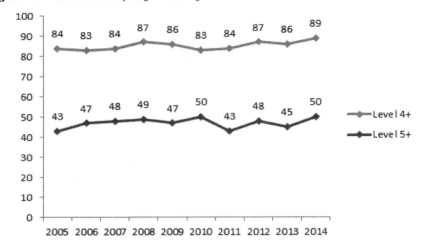

The 2006 PIRLS study (see Twist et al. 2007) showed that children in the UK tended to find reading less enjoyable than those in other countries and this was in line with findings from the 2001 survey. Twist et al. (2007: v) concluded:

> Attitudes to reading of 10-year-old children in England are poor compared to those of children in many other countries, and have declined slightly since 2001. Girls are generally more positive than boys. In England and most other countries, there is a positive association between attitude to reading and reading attainment.

As a result, Cremin et al. (2008a, b) surveyed teachers' reading habits, preferences and knowledge of children's literature. Their findings led them to conclude:

> It is debatable … whether teachers are familiar with a wide enough range of children's authors in order to plan richly integrated and holistic literacy work. (p. 458)

This chapter will examine what it means to be a reader and how teachers can develop both their pupils' and their own reading knowledge, skills and understanding. It will be argued that teachers have a key role not only in teaching the basic skills of reading, but also in motivating children to become real readers who view reading as a valuable life skill and a source of pleasure.

Research focus: Motivating readers

A project in New Zealand (Fletcher et al. 2012) examined ways in which children could be motivated to read. The study found that the following were key factors:

- Reading aloud to pupils and asking questions about the text

- Promoting books that might interest them, including encouraging the pupils to recommend books to each other
- Working on a one-to-one basis with the children to discuss their reading preferences
- Involving the parents

Cremin (2010: 6) maintained:

In order to motivate young readers, teachers need to balance literacy instruction, which tends to focus upon decoding and comprehension, with a reading for pleasure pedagogy, which focuses more upon engagement and response.

Pause for thought

- Do you read for pleasure? If so, which kinds of texts do you prefer?
- What strategies have you seen in schools which promote reading for pleasure?

Promoting reading for pleasure

Cremin (2010: 2) argued, *'Enticing invitations need to be offered to hear, read, inhabit, explore and respond to potent texts; such invitations have the potential to increase learners' confidence and their interest in reading'.*

There are simple things which teachers can do to promote engagement with literature. These include

Display excerpts from texts

When books begin to fall apart they can be dismembered and displayed. A labelled display featuring the cover, contents page, acknowledgements, publisher page, illustrations, and exciting excerpts can help children understand the anatomy of a book and provoke discussion. Similarly, displays of story openings or extracts from books can entice children to want to read more. Such extracts can also provide a stimulus for children's own writing.

A good read

BBC Radio 4's programme, A Good Read, features a group of people talking about stories they love and explaining why. Each panel member reads each of the recommendations so that a discussion can be held. This could be replicated with groups of children choosing favourite stories and could help broaden their knowledge of literature as well as helping them develop the ability to explore and respond to them.

Reading clubs

These can be formed within a class or across a year group or even a key stage. They can allow children to focus on one book as a group, with everyone reading the same section or the whole book and being prepared to discuss it in an informal group. Adult reading groups often enjoy refreshments as they chat and this might add to children's enjoyment.

Invite authors into school

Many children's authors enjoy sharing their books in schools and some, including the present author, do this on a voluntary basis. Children enjoy meeting someone who has written books and can talk about how they went about it and the challenges they faced. They can also engage in activities related to the stories, including writing predictions, short summaries of the story so far, character sketches, hot-seating and conscience alley, where a character has to make a decision in the story and receives conflicting advice from others.

Reading events

By celebrating occasions such as World Book Day, schools can highlight the importance of reading as well as the pleasure it can give. In 2017, a school in Devon held WBD events which included every teacher and child dressing as characters from well-known stories, and visits from children's authors who worked with classes and key stages. There were also opportunities to buy books and to take part in activities related to stories. Other schools have devised book days related to specific authors such as Roald Dahl, Michael Morpurgo and Anne Fine.

The Centre for Literacy in Primary Education (O'Sullivan and McGonigle 2010) ran a national project, *The Power of Reading*, and concluded that '*if children are given extended opportunities to explore texts in depth, they develop a deeper engagement, particularly in their empathy with characters and dilemmas*' (p. 58). The project confirmed the importance of the quality of illustrations, humour, links with popular culture, important themes and significant characters and found several examples of changes in children's motivation as readers.

Libraries

The *Libraries All Party Parliamentary Group* (2014) found there was a positive correlation between a good school library and attainment, achievement and motivation. These benefits were particularly strong for the most vulnerable students, including those from economically disadvantaged backgrounds. In some schools, libraries have been disbanded and books distributed to classrooms, with the space redeployed as, for example, a computer suite. This may restrict opportunities for children to explore a wide range of texts, including those which might not match their reading ages, but will match their interests and give them pleasure.

Visits to public libraries can be invaluable. Not only do libraries provide a rich source of literature, but they also often offer reading sessions led by librarians for visiting classes. Many children may be unaware that they can borrow books at no cost and can spend time exploring texts in comfort out of school hours, so giving them experience of libraries may encourage them to make greater use of them.

Displays of what we read

A good way to demonstrate the importance of reading in our everyday lives is to display pictures of the reading each of us does daily or weekly. Teachers could take

Figure 4.2 Examples of texts read by a teacher in a week

pictures of a collection of things they have read in a week, such as letters, cards, magazines, newspapers, novels, timetables and maps, as well as digital texts.

Whole classes could make displays such as reading rivers which show the flow of reading people do through a week. For examples, see http://www.journeys-fromimagestowords.com/teaching-tools.html

All of this could lead to discussions about the value of reading and the importance of being able to read a range of different types of texts as well as fiction, although it is important to recognize that fiction can be a powerful genre for cultivating an interest in reading.

Why fiction?

For some children and teachers, fiction is not the preferred reading choice. It is therefore worth examining the benefits of sharing fiction in school and of encouraging children to read and listen to stories. Given the preponderance of fiction in the texts we share with children, particularly when reading aloud to a class, it is important to consider the key benefits of fiction. These might include:

- Listening to stories being read by a skilled reader helps develop concentration and listening skills.
- The questions and discussions which accompany listening to stories help promote thinking, prediction and comprehension skills.
- Being exposed to a wide range of stories helps develop general knowledge. It takes us beyond our personal experiences and introduces us to new ideas and ways of thinking.
- Stories are an essential part of our cultural heritage: we relate events using storytelling techniques. We also use these techniques when relating events, telling jokes, explaining what happened in a film, play or TV programme, and even when giving evidence. An ability to sequence events, hold listeners' attention and entertain not only draws upon our language skills, but also makes us more able to interact in social situations.
- Listening to and reading stories expands our vocabularies and our knowledge of ways of using language.
- The knowledge of language we gain from stories helps us make our language more varied and interesting when we write.
- Experience of stories also provides ideas for scenarios when children write.
- By reading stories from a wide range of cultures we can improve our understanding of how people live in different societies and times.

- Discussing incidents from stories can promote discussion about moral issues and encourage children to consider how they would act in similar situations. As Goodwin has argued:

> At all stages of reading development, sharing the experience of a story enables children to understand more deeply and to tackle more complex ideas than they could alone. (Goodwin 2005: 49)

- Crucially, listening to and reading stories can be a highly pleasurable activity.

The social benefits of fiction have even been measured by researchers at the University of California, Berkeley. The study looked at a sample of ninety-four people and investigated the extent to which they read fiction and non-fiction. They then measured participants' social abilities by showing them videos and asking them questions about the mental states of people and asking them to match children to parents by looking at pictures. The research concluded that those participants who read more fiction demonstrated greater empathy and social awareness (Oatley 2008).

Reading to children

One of the best ways to engage children with literature is to share it with them by reading to them. Many educators welcomed the increased emphasis in the 2014 curriculum on reading to children, arguing that this had been neglected for some time in some schools and that this might account for a perceived decline in children's reading for pleasure (see PIRLS 2006). Not only are their benefits such as those cited above for exposure to stories, but it is also maintained that by reading to children teachers demonstrate that they value reading themselves.

It is interesting to note that the National Curriculum includes very similar guidance for each stage – Years 1–2, Years 3–4, Years 5–6:

> Pupils should continue to have opportunities to listen frequently to stories, poems, non-fiction and other writing, including whole books and not just extracts, so that they build on what was taught previously. In this way, they also meet books and authors that they might not choose themselves. (DfE 2013: 36)

In addition to all the educational justifications for reading stories to children, there is also the argument that doing so has benefits for class management and social cohesion, since the shared experience can be pleasant, often relaxing and sometimes tense, with the tension being shared by the group. Many teachers use story time as an incentive for children to behave well or focus upon other tasks (see Waugh 2015).

Chambers (1993) suggested strategies for making reading aloud more effective:

- Prepare – read the story several times, think about the key things you want to bring out, what the mood of the story is at different points and how you will convey this.

- Read picture books, non-fiction and poems as well as fiction. Pictures always enhance the interpretation of a text – don't confine them to KS1!
- Some children may like to follow the text – either in their own copies of the book or perhaps, if the text is relatively simple, onscreen. This will also help them to read it for themselves in due course.
- Encourage children to read aloud themselves – not as a task but for fun.
- Read aloud all through school years – and every day.

Pause for thought

- How confident do you feel about reading aloud to a class?
- What examples of good practice have you seen?

(See Chapter 8 for guidance on strategies for reading to children.)

Digital texts

It is important to recognize that much of the reading children experience outside school is presented in digital formats. Computer games, texts, emails, websites and social media form a major part of our reading diet and that of our pupils, and should also feature in their experience at school. Some schools have invested in devices such as Kindles and tablets so that children can read from screens. This can have distinct advantages for all children but particularly for some with learning difficulties or visual impairment, since text can be enlarged and background colours altered (see Chapter 3 for more detailed discussion about the use of digital and other texts).

Non-fiction

We may feel that it is obvious what comprises non-fiction: all texts which are not stories or poems. However, there is some debate about whether some texts can truly be defined as non-fiction. For example, some newspaper articles may be so slanted towards one political view that there might be said to be an element of fiction about them, while a campaigning leaflet, advertisement, tweet or blog may present one side of an argument and might make claims which are factually inaccurate. Some non-fiction writing is speculative and based upon limited evidence, such as the piece below.

Non-fiction genres were divided into distinct categories in the Primary Literacy Framework (DfEE 1998) and although this document is not current, it is worth looking at the main categories as a checklist for the experiences we offer our pupils.

Figure 4.3 A piece of writing about black holes created by Harry from Year 2 and Emily, a trainee teacher

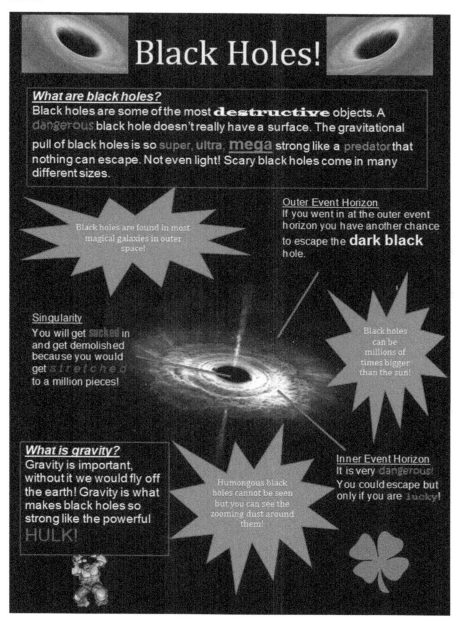

Figure 4.4 Writing produced by Ben from Year 4 and Jonathan, a trainee teacher

Discussion texts present a reasoned and balanced overview of an issue or controversial topic. Two or more different views on an issue are usually presented with evidence and/or examples provided to show why certain views are held.

Explanation texts explain how or why, for example, showing how and why hot air balloons work, or describing the rain cycle and explaining why it rains.

Instruction texts show how things should be done in order to achieve an outcome, for example, a recipe or guidance on how to make something or play a game.

Persuasive texts argue a case from a particular point of view in order to persuade readers to share the same point of view, for example manifestoes for elections and letters of complaint.

Non-chronological reports organize information in a range of different ways, but items are not presented in a chronological sequence as they might be in instruction texts. Texts could be presented in diagrams or charts like the one about black holes above or as a series of pieces of information like the one below.

Recount texts are designed to retell events and to inform and/or entertain, for example, a description of a journey or holiday or the story of a historical event.

Of course, we can get factual information from fiction writing too. Some stories, such as historical novels, include factual elements but make these more accessible to some readers by including them in a fictional or semi-fictional tale. Michael Morpurgo's *Private Peaceful*, for example, is a story but it is based upon the experiences of soldiers in the First World War and tells the reader a lot about the conditions in which they lived and fought.

The key to success might be summed up by Merisuo-Storm (2006: 112), who maintained.

> Pupils are very different as readers, and they are motivated to read very different books and texts. The reader should find the topic of the text interesting and possess enough previous knowledge related to its subject matter. Therefore it is crucial to offer pupils a wide variety of reading material. In other words, an array of books representing a variety of topics, levels of difficulty and genres of literature is necessary.

Poetry

There is a strong emphasis in the 2014 National Curriculum on the teaching and learning of poetry in both key stages. Children are expected to read and write poetry, learn it by heart, recognize it in different forms, perform and read it aloud and, of course, enjoy it.

However, Ofsted's *Poetry in Schools* report (Ofsted 2007) maintained that primary teachers' lack of knowledge of poetry was a key factor in inhibiting successful engagement with poetry. The report stated that poetry teaching was the weakest aspect of teaching of the English curriculum. Cremin et al. (2009), whose research on teachers and reading had revealed limitations in knowledge of children's books, also found that few teachers had sufficient knowledge and understanding to teach primary poetry effectively.

Perhaps the greatest problem for poetry in schools is that many teachers openly admit to disliking poetry. There is even a word for fear of poetry: *metrophobia.* This may arise because people had poor experiences of poetry in schools, perhaps because it was not read well or because their teachers lacked enthusiasm or understanding of the genre. However, poetry is part of everyday life, even if we do not always appreciate this. Think of a typical school day, which might include listening to songs on the radio on the way to work; singing hymns in assembly, and perhaps learning mnemonics as memory aids to recall points of the compass or the fates of Henry VIII's wives. In the playground, children may chant skipping rhymes, and in music there will be attention to lyrics. In the evening, you might watch a football match in which the crowd chant rhyming couplets (many of which could not be reproduced here!). And there may be adverts on TV which include rhymes. Poetry, and in particular, rhyme, is part of our culture and cannot be easily ignored. It is a powerful aid to memory – if you were asked to give an example of a spelling rule, you would almost certainly say: *i before e except after c,* even though this is a rule full of exceptions and there are many much more reliable ones which, unfortunately, do not have a rhyme.

Not only does poetry help develop children's sense of rhyme, but it also develops their phonemic awareness. Goswami (1990) found that pre-reading rhyming skills were a strong indicator of reading future development and acquisition of key reading skills. Bryant et al. (1990) tested 64 four to six-year-olds from different socioeconomic backgrounds on three occasions. They tested children's ability to detect rhyme at ages 4 years and 7 months and 5 years and 11 months, when they were asked to look at three words with pictures: two rhymed and the third did not (e.g. peg, cot, leg; fish, dish, book). They were asked to pick out the words which did not rhyme. At 6 years 7 months, children were given three different reading tests to assess the understanding of words and simple sentences, knowledge of frequent words, and spelling. There was a strong correlation between high scores in the rhyme test and scores in reading and spelling. Interestingly, this relationship was found regardless of the influence of the mother's educational level, and child's IQ and vocabulary level.

Whitehead (2007: 38) concurred, stating:

> Many poor readers are remarkably insensitive to rhymes and to the beginning sounds of words, but very young children with an interest in the sounds and poetry of language may well be on the road to reading, writing and spelling successfully.

With such evidence of the importance of exposing children to rhyme, it is important that we develop our ability to present poetry to children.

Sharing poetry and modelling

Rhyming poetry written for children is usually constructed in simple forms with a full-stop or comma at each line-break, and it is easy for children to get into the habit of stopping at the end of each line whether the sense demands it or not. The idea of *enjambement* – the use of phrases which go straight over a line-break in the poem – can be difficult for teachers and children to get used to. If we look at an example from T. S. Eliot's *The Waste Land*, we can see that pausing at the end of each line would make it difficult for listeners to understand the poem, but if we pause where there is punctuation, even when this is in the middle of a line, the poem makes much more sense.

> *April is the cruellest month, breeding*
> *Lilacs out of the dead land, mixing*
> *Memory and desire, stirring*
> *Dull roots with spring rain.*
> *Winter kept us warm, covering*
> *Earth in forgetful snow, feeding*
> *A little life with dried tubers.*

Try reading the lines below from Keats' *Endymion*:

> *A thing of beauty is a joy forever:*
> *Its loveliness increases; it will never*
> *Pass into nothingness but still will keep*
> *A bower quiet for us, and a sleep*
> *Full of sweet dreams, and health and quiet breathing.*

Many poets, including Shakespeare, make use of *enjambement*. If you have ever tried reading a Shakespearean play and found it difficult to comprehend, it maybe that it is not just the complexity of some of the language which is challenging, but the way you read the verse may be preventing you from understanding the text. This is one of the reasons why we find we can understand the plays much better when we see them performed by skilled actors who know where to pause and where to place emphasis on words or phrases.

It should be remembered that not all poetry rhymes and that there is a considerable variety of poetry which is suitable for children. The National Curriculum Programme of Study states that children should experience a range of classic and contemporary poetry, and that they should recognize forms of poetry such as free verse or narrative. The list below covers a range of poetic forms which might be used in the classroom:

● Nursery rhymes may be thought to be only for younger children, but older pupils might also study them to discover their origins and deeper meanings. For example, *Baa Baa Black Sheep* is about the thirteenth-century wool tax, while *Ring o' Roses* refers to the seventeenth-century Great Plague.

- Song lyrics are a rich source of rhyme and often interesting use of language and pronunciation. Most primary children take an interest in popular music and are aware of lyrics. Many folk songs tell stories of heroic or tragic events, while hymns and carols, which children sing regularly, are sometimes difficult to understand and could be interpreted and studied in lessons.

- Advertising jingles might be studied and children could come up with their own to advertise school events or sales.

- Rhyming mnemonics not only act as memory aids, but can be fascinating to study and invent or adapt. For example, the dubious *i before e except after c* is more reliable if the line *when the word rhymes with me* is added.

- Children are often asked to make cards for religious festivals, Mother's Day etc. Commercial versions could be displayed and children might be asked to produce their own.

- Comic verse can include short examples such as those written by Spike Milligan, as well as longer pieces by Roald Dahl, Hilarie Belloc, Michael Rosen, Allan Ahlberg, Kit Wright, Roger McGough and Pam Ayres.

- Narrative poetry not only engages children with a story, but also can provide a stimulus for discussion, drama and writing.

- Short, structured poems with a clear syllabic pattern such as limericks, haiku, cinquains and triolets illustrate how a message or poignant point can be conveyed in a few words. They also help develop children's understanding of rhythm, scansion and syllables.

- Free verse without rhyme can be a powerful medium of expression and is often easier for children to produce, since their creativity will not be inhibited by the need to find rhymes.

- Poetry which is often regarded as being written for adults, such as 'Ode to Autumn' by John Keats, the witches' brew in *Macbeth* by Shakespeare or 'Daffodils' by William Wordsworth, can be introduced at primary school, often using extracts to whet children's appetites for reading full versions.

- Poetry features in the literary heritage of most cultures and it is important to share examples with children, especially where classes are ethnically diverse.

- 'Nonsense' poems can engage and amuse, as well as making children think about vocabulary and phrasing. Probably the most used is *The Jabberwocky*, with its invented words which can be interpreted by using the context in which they are placed.

Poetry offers opportunities for performance, study of language and vocabulary, writing and discussion. It was described by Samuel Taylor Coleridge as being the best words in the best order and provides young writers with the chance to think carefully about vocabulary, structure and the effect their choices can have on readers.

Developing reading opportunities

For some children in key stage 1 and even beyond, reading is a chore: something to be done because you are in school. Such children may see little point in reading if it only involves struggling through reading schemes and simple texts while attempting to decode by matching letters to sounds. However, even beginner readers can be given meaningful reading activities which show them the value of being able to read. These might include simple treasure hunts with clues which include words which can be matched to lead to the next clue and eventually the 'treasure'. At first, text might be accompanied by pictures and single words such as table, shelf and box, but gradually prepositions can be added and pictures removed so that simple clues might be 'under the bin' or 'in the red box'. These can become increasingly sophisticated as children's reading develops and may even include rhymes or be created by older children or other children in the class.

Invented (or real) maps can be a good source for reading phonically regular words if place names are considered carefully. Children can add features such as railways, rivers, mountains and schools and can give them names. Maps of local areas and plans of the school can stimulate children and show them that through reading they can identify places.

Teachers as readers

O'Sullivan and McGonigle (2010) maintain that in order to engage and motivate children as readers teachers need a good knowledge of children's literature. Of course, primary teachers need a good knowledge of a wide variety of things in a wide range of subject areas, but if they are to engage children with reading then they open a window to all of those subject areas. As Cremin et al. (2008a) maintained:

> If teachers' enjoyment of reading can be extended to a wider range of authors, then this can only be beneficial for future readers whose diverse interests and reading preferences deserve to be both honoured and extended. (Cremin et al. 2008a: 19)

At the end of the chapter you will find details of organizations which provide resources and ideas for choosing and using books.

Research focus: Teachers as readers

Cremin et al. (2008a) looked at teachers as readers and studied primary teachers' personal reading, their knowledge of children's literature, their use of literature in the classroom, and their involvement in school library services.

Teachers were asked to name six children's authors, poets and picture book makers. The researchers concluded that

> it is questionable whether they know a sufficiently diverse range of writers to enable them to foster reader development and make informed recommendations to emerging readers with different needs and interests. The lack of professional knowledge and assurance with children's literature which this research reveals and the minimal knowledge of global literature indicated has potentially serious consequences for all learners, particularly those from linguistic and cultural minority groups who may well be marginalized unless teachers' own reading repertoires can be expanded. Furthermore, the infrequent mention of poetry in teachers' personal reading and their lack of knowledge of poets, as well as the relative absence of women poets and poets from other cultures writing in English, is also a concern, as is the dearth of knowledge of picture book creators, and the almost non-existent mention of picture book writers for older readers.
>
> It is debatable therefore whether teachers are familiar with a wide enough range of children's authors in order to plan richly integrated and holistic literacy work. The evidence suggests that if units of work or author studies are undertaken they are likely to be based around the work of writers from the canon, whose writing may already be very well known to children. The wide popularity and teacher reliance on the prolific work of Dahl may restrict children's reading repertoires, since child-based surveys suggest he is also a core author of choice for children. This convergence of choice by adults and children is likely to narrow the range still further. (p. 458)

Pause for thought

- Could you name six children's authors, poets and picture book makers?
- Which children's authors' work do you know well?
- Do you ever read poetry for pleasure rather than just as part of your work?

CASE STUDY: Creating a school children's literature portfolio

Working in a small school with 120 pupils, Emily was given responsibility for literacy in her second year of teaching. She wanted to begin by engaging all staff in an activity which would involve sharing expertise and knowledge as well as benefiting staff and pupils so she shared the children's literature portfolio she had produced when she was a student teacher and suggested that the teachers and teaching assistants create one for the whole school.

The objective was to share knowledge of a range of different children's stories and poems and to provide lesson ideas related to the texts and links to the National Curriculum. After discussion with the headteacher, Emily decided that busy teachers would be more likely to contribute useful entries if time were set aside for them to do so. The project was explained at a staff meeting and staff were asked to look at and bring along one story and one poem to a CPD session the following week. They were also to bring laptops and copies of the National Curriculum.

Each story or poem was to have a brief description followed by comments about how it might be used in the classroom. Staff were encouraged to find ways in which texts might enhance learning across the curriculum as well as in English lessons. Once notes had been made they were discussed with colleagues from the same key stage before being shared with the whole group. There were many suggestions for other stories and poems which could be added to the portfolio and the deputy headteacher offered to put finished entries into a section of the school website so that everyone could access it wherever they were working on planning.

The headteacher discussed the literature portfolios at a cluster meeting for heads and three other schools asked if they could get involved. As a result, a cluster portfolio was developed which was contributed to and drawn upon by several schools. Below you will find two examples of portfolio entries: one for a novel and one for a poem.

Marie's entry

Figure 4.5 Literature portfolio entry on a novel

Title: 'Girls Can't Play Football!'   Author: David Waugh

Genre: Fiction   Sub-genre: Realist/adventure

Figure 4.5 Continued

Comment:

A book very relevant to the gender stereotypes of modern Britain. Although we live in a modern society, issues of inequality still exist and this book deals with them via the type of adventure story that usually has a male protagonist and is aimed at boys. Girls are now encouraged to play football and join local teams, but there does still exist an attitude that girls can't play football as well as boys. This book not only challenges these attitudes, but also has the sub-plot of an adventure story running through it and would appeal to both boy and girl readers. Interestingly, though it is never a factor in the storyline and there is no mention of it throughout the book, the final illustration shows that the central character is black. This might lead to some discussion. Would it have been relevant to mention Lauren's skin colour? If she had been white, would her skin colour have been mentioned? The story shows the irrelevance of skin colour and race to a plot, focusing instead on a key area of prejudice: sexism.

Suitable for Key Stage 2.

Relevance to literacy lessons:

Characterization – there are several strong characters in this book. Are some of them clichéd and stereotyped or is the stereotype subverted? (Nerdy school boy/bully/hero/villain)

Setting – how is the realistic setting portrayed? How does the school setting in this book compare with school settings in other books?

Speech and dialogue – different speech patterns for different characters.

Links to National Curriculum:

Key Stage 2.

Pupils should be taught to:

Read books that are structured in different ways; identify themes and conventions in a wide range of books; discuss words and phrases that capture the reader's imagination and interest; ask questions to improve their understanding of the text; draw inferences from characters' feelings, thoughts and motives; identify how language, structure and presentation contribute to meaning; participate in discussions about books, taking turns and listening to what others have to say; discuss and evaluate how authors use language, considering the impact on the reader; prepare poems and plays to read aloud and to perform, showing understanding through intonation, tone and volume so that the meaning is clear to an audience.

Relevance to other areas of the curriculum:

PSHE – gender/race/inequality/ being a team player

PE – sports games related to football.

The National Curriculum for physical education aims to ensure that all pupils:

Develop competence to excel in a broad range of physical activities; are physically active for sustained periods of time; engage in competitive sports and activities; lead healthy active lives.

Science – health and diet of sportspeople and relevance to the foods we eat. Effect of exercise on the body. Do girls have as much physical stamina as boys – can we prove/disprove this. Should mixed teams be an option for the future? Which sport takes the greatest toll on a human body?

IT + History – research the history of women's football in the UK and worldwide.

Links to National Curriculum:

Key Stage 2.

Pupils should be taught to:

Changes within living memory – these should be used to reveal aspects of change in national life; the Roman Empire and its impact on Britain; a study of a theme or aspect in British history that extends pupils' chronological knowledge beyond 1066.

Nick's entry

Figure 4.6 Literature portfolio entry on a poem

Poem Information:			Poem:
Title: The Robot Author: David Waugh Classification: Poetry			It whirrs and clicks all day long, But has never broken down. It always makes my breakfast Without a smile or frown.
Subject	Curriculum Link	Activity	And when I'm ready to go to school, It carefully cleans my teeth.
English	'draft and write by: organising paragraphs around a theme'	Children could try and create a poem from another person in the poem's perspective. Each paragraph or stanza will need to include a different activity.	You see, the things my robot does Are quite beyond belief! We walk to school hand in hand.
English	'draft and write by: in narratives, creating settings, characters and plot'	Children could write the robot's version of the day. Writing about other activities that he could do for the reader. If they had a robot for the day what would they do?	The other children stare. Nobody ever bullies me. I don't think that they'd dare. My robot is two metres tall And does whatever I say. It waits for me outside the school
Mathematics	'measure, compare add and subtract: lengths, mass, volume'	Children could look into the length of the robot. How much bigger is the robot than them? How much bigger is it than a car?	Until the end of day. It sends me secret messages By radio all day long. I don't think that my teacher knows Why I never get sums wrong!
Science	'construct a simple series of electrical circuit, identifying and naming its basic parts'	Children could look into circuits and how having a complete circuit allows something to work. They would look into building their own robot to perform a simple action.	It has to hide at playtime. The teachers won't let it stay. They say that it's just too big And gets in everyone's way. I really like my robot
Computing	'understand what algorithms are; how they are implemented as programs'	Using a Romer device, get the children to write an algorithm to draw the robot. They will need to think about the appropriate size of its arms compared to its body.	It's quite my favourite toy, And do you know, I've no idea If it's a girl or boy.
Art	'to develop a wide range of art and design techniques in using colour, pattern, texture, line, shape, form and space'	Children could look into different materials, techniques of getting a metallic appearance. They could create a portrait of the robot using this.	
Design & Technology	'understand and use electrical systems in their products'	Children could look into other types of robots and how we use them in day to day life. What makes a robot work?	

Pause for thought

- How could you develop your knowledge of stories and poems while helping plan for literacy lessons?
- Could you start your own children's literature portfolio and develop it as a resource as your career progresses?

Summary

This chapter has looked at what is involved in being a reader. It means understanding that there are many different types of text and being able to enjoy and engage with them. Teachers have a vital role, both through being knowledgeable about different genres and through modelling reading. In Chapter 4 we looked at the skills needed for reading and in this chapter the focus has been on putting those skills into practice. It is worth looking at a diagram which draws the various aspects of reading together and gives teachers a way of looking at their pupils' abilities and gauging their abilities and needs.

Scarborough's Reading Rope shows that there are multiple strands to reading. Like the Simple View of Reading, it has two main strands: word recognition and language comprehension. It then subdivides these into sub-strands that need to 'become entwined' as pupils learn to coordinate the different components of reading.

Figure 4.7 Adaptation or Scarborough's Reading Rope by EEF (2017)

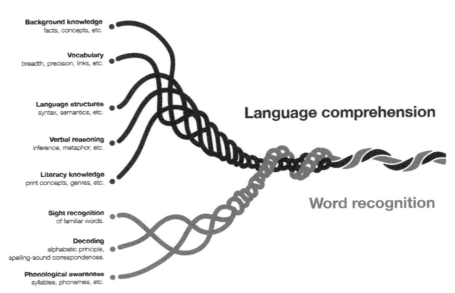

It should be remembered that children (and adults) may be more successful in some of the elements for some texts than for others. Even skilled readers with excellent word recognition and decoding skills can be challenged when reading texts which include topics of which they have little understanding with vocabulary which may be decodable, but is not easily comprehensible. Being a reader means having strategies which will make most texts accessible. It also means being an active reader who engages with texts rather than simply being a person who can decode text.

From reading this chapter you should have a clearer understanding of:

- What it means to be a reader and how teachers can develop both their pupils' and their own reading skills and understanding.

- The key role that teachers play, not only in teaching the basic skills of reading, but also in motivating children to become real readers who view reading as a valuable life skill and a source of pleasure.

- Ways of making reading an attractive and engaging activity for children.

- The importance of engaging children with poetry as well as stories, digital texts and non-fiction.

Recommended reading

For discussion about children's fiction and ideas for the classroom see:

Gamble, N. (2012). *Exploring Children's Literature: Reading with Pleasure and Purpose*. London: Sage.

Graham, J. (2004). *Cracking Good Books. Teaching Literature at Key Stage One*. Sheffield: NATE.

Grainger, T., Goouch, K. and Lambirth, A. (2005). *Creative Activities for Plot, Character and Setting*. Leamington Spa: Scholastic.

Martin, T. et al. (2004). *The Really Useful Literacy Book. Being Creative with Literacy in the Primary Classroom*. London: Routledge Falmer.

Waugh, D. and Neaum, S. eds. (2013). *Beyond Early Reading*. London: Critical Publishing.

Waugh, D., Neaum, S. and Waugh, R. (2016). *Children's Literature in Primary Schools*. London: Sage.

For discussion about non-fiction and ideas for the classroom see:

Allott, K. 'Non-fiction writing' in Waugh, D., Neaum, S. and Bushnell, A. eds. (2015). *Beyond Early Writing*. Northwich: Critical Publishing.

Organizations which provide useful resources

The Centre for Literacy in Primary Education (www.clpe.org.uk) offer highly respected CPD training, resources and book packs. Their website includes free core book lists (www.clpe.org.uk/corebooks), as well as themed lists and books of the week.

The UK Literacy Association (www.ukla.org) offers a range of resources including *Building Communities of Readers*, a CPD booklet to help teachers develop as 'reading teachers' and to record children's attitudes. It includes detailed outlines of sessions that support teachers to

- Develop their knowledge of children's authors and books
- Plan and sustain opportunities for children to read independently for pleasure
- Read aloud
- Plan regular book promotion activities
- Make individual and whole-class book recommendations
- Reflect on their personal reading histories
- Develop mutually beneficial relationships with families and libraries and build on children's out of school reading experiences.

The National Literacy Trust (www.literacytrust.org.uk) provides a wealth of useful research and practice materials. Their *Literacy Guide for Primary Schools* and *Annual Literacy Review* both contain sections on reading for pleasure. They also produce a staff meeting PowerPoint resource, *Building Our Knowledge of Quality Children's Literature*.

Letterbox Library (www.letterboxlibrary.com) is a children's bookseller specializing in books which celebrate equality, diversity and inclusion. They ensure that everything they sell is inclusive since if all children are to engage with books and reading it is vital that they are given opportunities to find themselves in stories. All of their books have been preselected by a team of reviewers which includes teachers, librarians and children. They have put together a booklist especially for this resource and you can find it at www.teachers.org.uk/reading-for-pleasure.

Chapter 5
Skills to Develop in English: The Four Modes of Language

Chapter objectives

This chapter will:

- Examine the skills involved in becoming proficient speakers, listeners, readers and writers
- Analyse the elements of vocabulary, spelling, grammar and punctuation and how to teach these in creative ways
- Review research studies into developing the skills in learning English
- Cite case studies of schools that are explicitly teaching the skills to exemplify developing mastery in contextualized ways

Pupils should be taught to control their speaking and writing consciously and to use Standard English. This should be taught to use the elements of spelling, grammar, punctuation and language about language listed. This is not intended to constrain or restrict teachers' creativity, but simply to provide the structure on which they can construct exciting lessons. (The National Curriculum in England, DfE 2013: 16)

Introduction

The extract above from the National Curriculum Framework emphasizes that the skills related to English need to be explicitly taught; however, the danger is that this could lead to an approach that decontextualizes these and which could act as a disincentive for children to engage in English lessons. As Chapter 3 has made very clear, this should not be the case. English should be an 'irresistible activity', with lessons that are relevant and over which children have ownership and control. The National Curriculum acknowledges that the teaching of skills should not 'restrict teachers' creativity' in providing 'exciting lessons', but the challenge is how to achieve this. This chapter will provide guidance on teaching the skills of speaking, listening, reading and writing and the related elements of grammar, spelling, vocabulary and punctuation. It will highlight that speaking and listening are at the heart of becoming a good reader and writer and will put considerable emphasis upon this. The chapter will examine the different aspects of skills that underpin all four modes of language, and emphasize the importance integrating them to create engaging contextualized English units of work. This should help ensure that creativity is not lost in the process.

Speaking and listening

Speaking and listening are skills that are central to our lives as they enable us to communicate thoughts, feelings and experiences. Children who have delayed or impaired language can suffer significant disadvantages in being able to communicate and this is likely to impact on their ability to become effective readers and writers. The Bercow Report (2008) drew national attention to the *'grossly inadequate recognition across society of the importance of communication development, let alone the active steps needed to facilitate it'* (Bercow 2008: 16). It is therefore vital that teachers understand the need to develop proficient spoken language and know how to facilitate it. The National Curriculum acknowledges this:

> The national curriculum for English reflects the importance of spoken language in pupils' development across the whole curriculum – cognitively, socially and linguistically. (DfE 2013: 14)

This is also reflected in Ofsted's (2016) inspection framework which stresses the importance of children being able to articulate their knowledge and understanding.

The dynamic nature of speaking and listening

In understanding key aspects of speaking and listening, it is first important to appreciate its dynamic nature and its fundamental difference from written language. Luoma (2004) sets out the features of spoken discourse:

- Units of ideas (phrases or clauses)
- Either planned or spontaneous in nature
- Uses more vague or generic words than written language (such as 'thingy', etc.)
- Uses fixed phrases, hesitation and fillers (such as 'like' or 'um', 'er' 'and so on')
- Often contains errors, reflecting the ongoing processing of the speaker's thoughts
- Involves reciprocity and is a form of interaction

- Varies to reflect the role of the speaker, the purpose and the context
- Contains conversation routines such as greetings or farewells
- Adopts different styles according to the purpose and context

The Australian First Steps resource for speaking and listening reinforces this:

> As speaking and listening is dependent on the context in which it is embedded, students need to be taught about situational and socio-cultural contexts. That is the purpose of the speaking and listening, the audience involved and the situation in which the speaking and listening is taking place. (First Steps 2013: 5)

First Steps describes this process as 'dynamic' as speakers and listeners interact to construct meaning. This extensive resource includes a model to help understand this (see page 7: http://det.wa.edu.au/stepsresources/detcms/navigation/first-steps-literacy/). During the process, speakers and listeners make choices about how they will speak and listen according to particular contexts.

Progression in speaking and listening

The National Curriculum states,

> Pupils should be taught to speak clearly and convey ideas confidently using Standard English. They should learn to justify ideas with reasons; ask questions to check understanding; develop vocabulary and build knowledge; negotiate; evaluate and build on the contributions of others; and select the appropriate register for effective communication. They should be taught to give well-structured descriptions and explanations and develop their understanding through speculating, hypothesising and exploring ideas. This will enable them to clarify their thinking as well as organise their ideas for writing. (DfE 2013: 10)

However, no specific guidance on progression in spoken language is provided in the latest curriculum. If teachers are to ensure pupils achieve mastery in the range of aspects detailed above, they need to know what progression looks like and how to plan and support it. A resource produced by the Primary National Strategy: Speaking, Listening, Learning (DfES 2003) examined the features of progression for years 1–6 for the areas of speaking, listening, group interaction and drama, and is still helpful in providing guidance on the features of progression. Another useful resource for understanding progression in oral language development is the recently updated 'First Steps Speaking and Listening Map of Development' (Education Department of Western Australia 2013). This guidance, together with the accompanying resource book, provides key indicators of the different phases, major teaching emphases for each phase (there are seven delineated) and suitable teaching and learning experiences. These useful resources, which although described as related to Standard Australian English, have wider application and are available to download from: http://det.wa.edu.au/stepsresources/detcms/navigation/first-steps-literacy/.

The phases consist of:

Phase 1: beginning – In this phase, children use the language of the home and community to communicate with familiar others. They often rely on non-verbal cues to convey and comprehend spoken language. Their speech may be characterized by short utterances and they may require support in unfamiliar settings.

Phase 2: early – In this phase, students use their own variety of English language to communicate needs, express ideas and ask questions. They understand spoken language relating to personal and social interests and respond in their own way. They are becoming aware of appropriate ways of interacting in familiar situations.

Phase 3: exploratory – In this phase, students use Standard [Australian] English effectively within familiar contexts. They communicate appropriately in both structured and unstructured situations. They explore ways of using language for different speaking and listening purposes.

Phase 4: consolidating – In this phase, students use most language structures and features of Standard [Australian] English appropriately when speaking in a range of contexts. They show increasing awareness of the needs of their audience. They experiment with ways to adjust listening and speaking to suit different purposes.

Phase 5: conventional – In this phase, students recognize and control most language structures and features of Standard [Australian] English when speaking for a range of purposes. They select and sustain language and style appropriate to audience and purpose. They are aware of the value of planning and reflecting to improve the effectiveness of communication.

Phase 6: proficient – In this phase, students' control of Standard [Australian] English reflects their understanding of the way language structures and features are manipulated to achieve different purposes and effects. They evaluate the appropriateness and effectiveness of spoken texts in relation to audience, purpose and context. They experiment with complex devices to improve their communication.

Phase 7: advanced – In this phase, students show a sophisticated control of Standard [Australian] English in a range of contexts. They understand the power and effect of spoken language, critically analysing factors that influence the interpretation of spoken texts. They use complex devices to modify and manipulate their communication for a range of purposes.

(Education Department of Western Australia 2013: vi–vii).

Teaching strategies to support speaking and listening

Based on an understanding of progression in speaking and listening, teachers need to be able to use appropriate teaching strategies to support pupils in developing mastery. One of the most important, and often neglected, aspects is to develop an ability to be a good listener. Too often, pupils are asked to listen, but have not fully understood, what good listening entails. This is true of adults too, especially in the current climate of so many ways of distracting our attention, so that email, messaging and social media can absorb a significant amount of our time and attention. Being a good role model for children in what good listening, or active listening looks like is vital. The next section examines a case study of explicitly teaching active listening. It is important to bear in mind that

> listening is more than hearing; it is an interactive process obtaining information for pleasure and for building relationships.
>
> (Education Department of Western Australia 2013: 5)

CASE STUDY: Active listening

In one primary school in the North East of England a key focus was on ensuring pupils developed the skills of working together cooperatively. This entails teaching the interpersonal and small-group skills required. A fundamental skill is to ensure pupils become proficient at active listening. At the beginning of each school year, across the school, a focus is given to this and then revisited during the year. The steps used, while done in different ways for different age groups, consist of:

1 *Establishing the need for active listening*: this is done through role-play. First the teacher and another adult model what poor active listening looks like and the impact of it. The children enjoy watching the teachers 'behaving badly' (e.g. showing lack of eye contact, bored body language (yawning, etc.), fiddling with other objects)! Pairs of children work together to discuss what is wrong with it and what active listening should look like. Children are selected to role-play good active listening using drama techniques such as forum theatre where a small group acts out a scene while the rest of the class watches them. The class work as directors of the group in role, for example asking them to act or speak in a different way.

2 *Define the skill*: in this stage the teacher uses a 'T chart' (draws a large T on the board or large piece of paper with either side of the T marked 'sounds like' and 'looks like'). With older children, a double 'T chart' is used showing also what it feels like (see Figure 5.1 for an example). The teacher works with the class to discuss what they might put in each column to show what the skill sounds like and looks like or feels like. The children then work in small groups to construct their own chart. Following asking groups to 'roam the room' to view each other's charts, one is selected to form a poster in the classroom to be used for constant reference while the skill is practised and refined.

3 *Provide guided practice*: here the teacher ensures that there are plenty of opportunities for pupils to practise the skill with corrective feedback. Using a skill of the week to focus on, (in this example, active listening), the teacher monitors, observes, intervenes, coaches, reinforces and encourages pupils while they are working in pairs and groups to demonstrate good active

listening. Pupils reflect on how well they practised the skill and how they could become more effective. The teacher rewards good listening through awarding team points each day to the best groups or pairs.

4 *Ensure generalized application of the skill*: once the skill has been established, the teacher provides opportunities for using the skill in a range of contexts, showing it is valued and good active listening is celebrated.

Following this explicit teaching, a common language was developed throughout the school to demonstrate good active listening. Marked improvements were seen in the behaviour of children generally and this was also a positive way of stressing expected behaviour in lessons.

Figure 5.1 Active Listening T chart
Source: Author, images from copyright free images available on internet

Active Listening		
Looks like 	**Sounds like** 	**Feels like** 

Pause for thought

- Why do you think the stages described in the case study are necessary to teach active listening?
- Why is role-play a useful strategy here?
- What are the advantages of explicit modelling of both poor and good active listening?

Research focus

Coultas (2016) details three case studies of teachers during 'critical moments' in a lesson to demonstrate teachers' knowledge about talk. Based on a social-constructivist perspective on learning originating from Vygotsky (1978:89) that '*human learning is specifically social in nature*', Coultas argues that this requires the teacher to use the social situation of the classroom effectively. Coultas notes, '*This idea of a critical moment for talk built on Tripp's (1993) idea of a critical incident in teaching where a teacher look backs and analyses a key moment in professional practice to reflect on and evaluate practice in closer detail*' (2016: 33). Using video of lessons where teachers had planned to incorporate talk for learning, they watched these and selected a critical moment. Together with the researcher, these were analysed to note strengths, constraints and challenges and particularly interesting features. This proved an effective means of promoting reflection and demonstrating teachers' knowledge and understanding of talk for learning. One of the findings, perhaps predictably, was that

> the standards rhetoric, that is highly outcomes and exam oriented, puts pressure on teachers to use more traditional methods of teacher talk, reinforcing didactic methods to drill students to get the grades. (Coultas 2013: 37)

All the teachers noted that talk was not a priority in a 'test culture'. What the case studies did illustrate is that making teachers more aware of their practice can be positive in triggering critical reflection and improving practice.

Pause for thought

- How useful is video in stimulating a deeper reflection on teaching?
- Why is talk often marginalized in the classroom?
- How might different teaching approaches stimulate effective talk for learning?

Philosophy for Children

Philosophy for Children (P4C) was developed in the 1960s as a response to a concern about a lack of reasoning and dialogic skills among undergraduate students (Gregory 2008). The scheme was expanded for primary and secondary schools to improve reasoning, creativity, personal and interpersonal skills and ethical understanding. Teachers employ Socratic questioning to encourage pupils '*to seek clarification, probe reasons and evidence, explore alternative views, test implications and consequences and ask questions about the question*' (Fisher 2003: 154–5). Fisher (2012) claims this supports children's thinking skills and that children as young as five years can engage in philosophical questioning. Research also shows that it impacts on academic achievement (Trickey and Topping 2004; Fisher 2005). The common lesson format includes ten steps as follows:

Step 1: Preparation. Here a focusing exercise or thinking activity or game or a relaxation exercise helps gain the children's attention and gets them in the right frame of mind.

Step 2: Sharing a stimulus: presenting a story, poem or picture or other stimulus for thinking that aims to promote a creative or imaginative response.

Step 3: Thinking time: children consider what is unusual or interesting about the stimulus and share this with a partner or in a small group.

Step 4: Questioning: children work together to devise questions.

Step 5: Question airing: questions are recorded to be shared

Step 6: Question choosing: selection from the class questions can be done in a variety of ways including voting.

Step 7: First thought: here the children who devised the chosen question share their thinking behind this question.

Step 8: Building: teachers use Socratic questioning to model and prompt pupils. The dialogue should be reciprocal, cumulative and supportive.

Step 9: Last thoughts: an opportunity for all pupils to share any further thoughts on the subject.

Step 10: Review: this is an opportunity to collectively assess how well they worked together in a community of enquiry.

For a range of teaching resources, see www.P4C.com.

O'Riordan (2016: 657) notes from a study of a sample of teachers' practice in using P4C:

> The implementation of philosophical enquiry challenged teachers' understanding of what constitutes good teaching and learning in the classroom as dictated by the culture of accountability and control.

One of the study's conclusions was that in such a climate '*P4C is a counter-cultural practice*' (O'Riordan 2016: 654). One of the key factors is that in such a climate of accountability, teachers need sustained support to develop different approaches. Another approach to learning, cooperative learning, referred to in Chapter 2, is also predicated on talk for learning. The next section provides an overview, but also stresses the importance of ongoing support for teachers in order to develop it. None of these pedagogical approaches are 'quick fixes': they rely on a deep understanding of the theoretical and research base and a phased method of implementation.

Cooperative group work

In Chapter 2 the links between a mastery approach and cooperative learning were explored. Cooperative learning is not just 'group work' and requires certain factors to be present for it to be genuinely 'cooperative'. Research demonstrates that when implemented properly, cooperative learning presents an ideal method of supporting not only children's learning, but also the effective use of talk (Johnson and Johnson 1989; Slavin 1995; Sharan 1990; Jenkins et al. 2003; Kyndt et al. 2013). As with Philosophy for Children, cooperative learning requires careful implementation beginning with developing a depth of understanding and also experiencing cooperative learning in any professional development teachers undertake. This should be followed by peer support and recursive opportunities to enhance understanding and support application in the classroom. Johnson and Johnson (in press) have described this process as 'master, retain, transfer'. Jolliffe's study into implementation (2015) found that schools, working together, with a community of facilitators, or experts, to provide support, 'bridged the gap' between the promise and actual use of cooperative learning in the classroom. (For further information on a phased approach to implementing cooperative learning, see Jolliffe 2007.)

The first step in developing cooperative learning in the classroom is to ensure that pupils are supported with the necessary interpersonal and small-group skills to cooperate, including active listening as detailed previously. The other key skills include task skills and working relationship skills as follows:

Task skills are focused on the content of the task and include:

1 Generating and elaborating on ideas
2 Following instructions
3 Staying on task
4 Managing time successfully
5 Planning and reviewing progress

Working relationship skills are focused on positive relationships in the group and include:

1 Helping and encouraging each other
2 Everyone participating
3 Showing appreciation
4 Reaching agreement

The second step is to structure the tasks to maximize the potential to cooperate. One of the key aspects is to ensure that pupils are interdependent, or what is termed 'positive interdependence' (Johnson and Johnson 1999). They also need to be individually accountable for their share of the task. Using a range of cooperative learning strategies, or what Kagan (1994) calls 'structures', can support this process. The most common of these are 'think-pair-share', 'rally table', 'line up', 'three-step interview', 'two stay and two stray' and 'jigsaw groups' but there are estimated to be over 200 of these classroom structures. For further guidance, see Kagan (1994) and www.kaganonline.com. You will also find many ideas for cooperative learning structures on Pinterest: https://uk.pinterest.com.

Dialogic teaching

Another approach that centres on talk is dialogic teaching. Following Alexander's (2000) comparative research of primary education across five countries, he developed the concept of 'dialogic teaching' which aims to harness the power of talk to stimulate and extend pupils' thinking and understanding. Dialogic teaching consists of the following five elements (Alexander 2004):

- It is *collective*: children work together on tasks, as a group or class.
- It is *reciprocal*: teachers and children listen to each other and comment/share ideas.
- It is *supportive*: children are supported to discuss their views freely.
- It is *cumulative*: teachers and children build on each other's ideas to create coherent lines of thinking.
- It is *purposeful*: teachers plan and steer classroom talk with specific purposes.

Just as P4C and cooperative learning require sustained support to be implemented successfully, dialogic teaching also requires considerable time and effort to be effective as it is '*in effect a transformation of the culture of talk and the attendant assumptions about the relationship of teacher and taught*' (Alexander 2005: 16).

Dialogic teaching, cooperative learning and Philosophy for Children are three key approaches to learning and teaching that can ensure that speaking and listening are given the focus they require in both developing the vital skills of effective communication and in supporting the learning process. It is also important to consider the use of questioning and consider carefully the inclusion of open questions during teaching. As discussed in Chapter 3, drama is also a rich resource that will support authentic speaking and listening activities. The case studies cited in Chapter 3 also demonstrates that talk is at the heart of creative approaches to learning.

Pause for thought – *Planning speaking and listening opportunities*

Consider a lesson you are planning for a specific age group and how to ensure that it has a speaking focus. You will find the Communication Trust 'No Pens Wednesday' initiative a useful resource for ideas: a resource activity pack to support this initiative is available at https://www.thecommunicationtrust.org.uk/projects/no-pens-day-wednesday/

You can also find resources from TES online at https://www.tes.com/teaching-resource/no-pens-day-primary-lesson-plans-6215889
Review the following questions:

- What will be the focus of the activity – talk as interaction, transaction or performance?
- How will the activity be modelled?
- What stages will the activity be divided into?
- What language support will be needed?
- What resources will be needed?
- How and when will feedback be given?

Research study

A study by Westgate and Hughes (2015, 2016) reports on a project with six schools to improve learning through speaking and listening. The schools involved acknowledged a dilemma:

> They realise that the way to develop the reading and writing of thoughtful, imaginative and reflective texts is through encouraging children's creativity, understanding and imagination. They are also clear that children's creativity and imagination can be fostered by discussion and interaction; yet in a tightly controlled curriculum they have wondered how to find time to provide opportunities for the development of S & L, even though these underpin both literacy and general curricular progress. (2015: 566)

The schools in the project sought to answer this dilemma through improving the learning and teaching of speaking and listening. They received half a day's training per term, plus the ongoing support from a consultant. Teachers were also given some flexibility in approach, but many opted for cooperative group work as a vehicle for supporting talk for learning. A further feature was ownership by children and their awareness of '*how productive dialogue may be managed has been a prominent theme*' (2015: 575). The study showed that the skills can be effectively taught and that '*they will transfer across contexts when teaching is of a dialogic nature*' (2015: 1). The project used explicit teaching of spoken language such as the ability to give well-structured descriptions and explanations and communication skills such as reaching a consensus, disagreeing politely, building on the contributions of others as well as developing understanding, such as using evidence to justify reasoning and/or points of view. In conclusion '*The work of the six teachers in the present study demonstrates multiple benefits for their children*' (2015: 574).

Pause for thought

- Consider the importance of explicitly teaching skills of spoken language and communication in this study.
- Why was dialogic teaching an important feature?
- In what ways did using cooperative learning support this focus?

Reading

The skills involved in the teaching of reading principally relate to two areas: word recognition and language comprehension. Set against a background of continued debate about the importance of different aspects, and particularly the role of phonics in the teaching of reading, a number of models have been developed by researchers and experts in the field to help deconstruct the elements involved in becoming a proficient reader. The most common model is known as the 'Simple View of Reading' (Gough and Tunmer 1986) – see Figure 5.2. This focuses on two components: *decoding* and *comprehension*. Decoding means the ability to recognize words out of context and to apply phonic rules to this recognition; thus it is termed 'word recognition'. Comprehension means linguistic comprehension, which is

Figure 5.2 The Simple View of Reading
Source: DfES (2006) Independent Review of the Teaching of Early Reading (Final Report by Jim Rose). Ref: 0201/2006DOC-EN. Nottingham: DfES Publications, p. 40

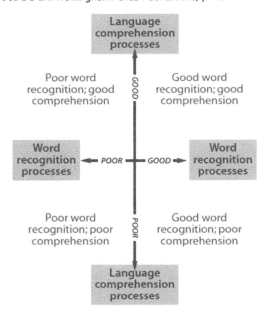

defined by Gough and Tunmer (1986) as the process by which words, sentences and discourse are interpreted. They also state that the two interrelated processes are both necessary for reading. This model has been developed since first proposed in 1986, and became widely known and advocated in the Rose Review (*Independent Review of the Teaching of Early Reading*) (DfES 2006b: 77). Stuart and Stainthorp (2016: 35) note that '*all contemporary models of reading are dual-route models*' and that while there is disagreement about the details or the relative importance or each, most acknowledge there are two sets of processes: language comprehension and word recognition.

Skills related to word recognition

There are two aspects involved in word recognition. One is being able to map the letters to the sounds, known as grapheme/phonemes correspondence and blend these for reading, or more commonly called the teaching of phonics. The second is being able to develop fast recognition of common irregular words, or *common exception words* as they are termed in the 2014 National Curriculum. While most high-frequency irregular words, such as 'was', 'said' and 'the', can be decoded using phonics, the phonic rules to enable this to be done are more complex and taught in later stages. But of course, children need these words early on and therefore most phonics schemes, such as *Letters and Sounds* (DfES 2007a), introduce a limited number of these words to be read as whole words, alongside teaching a systematic programme of grapheme/phoneme correspondences.

1. Phonics

The teaching of phonics is a statutory part of the National Curriculum and schools have to report the progress of children at age six, using the phonics screening check. This has led to much debate and a focus on phonics by schools, sometimes to the detriment of the other important aspects (Dombey 2011; Davies 2012). Understanding the role of phonics in the teaching of reading is therefore an important starting point.

The role of phonics

As theoretical models of teaching reading demonstrate, one key element in effective reading is the ability to decode unfamiliar words. Phonics provides the key to unlocking the alphabetic code, as detailed below, and being able to map the grapheme/phoneme correspondences, or letters to sounds, is a skill that supports reading and spelling. The integrated processes of word recognition and language comprehension are equally important. Learning phonics supports the decoding element and it is important to note that teaching phonics alone will not produce good readers – children need to develop skills in both key areas.

The alphabetic code

The alphabetic code refers to the concept that letters, or combinations of letters, are used to represent the sounds of our language. English has a complex alphabetic code as there are 26 letters and yet approximately 44 sounds. The correspondence between the letters (the graphemes) and the sounds (the phonemes) is inconsistent, which has led to a reluctance to use phonics for teaching reading in English, unlike other languages which are more consistent. Using the International Phonetic Alphabet can be helpful as a reference tool (see the National Curriculum, Appendix 1, p. 74). There are four principles that help explain the complex English alphabetic code:

1 Sounds/phonemes are represented by letters/graphemes.

2 A phoneme can be represented by one or more letters, for example the phoneme /aɪ/ can be written as 'i' (in tiger), 'i-e' (in line) or 'igh' (in sight). A one-letter grapheme is called a graph, a two-letter grapheme, a digraph, and a three letter grapheme, a trigraph, and occasionally there are four-letter graphemes, quadgraphs, (as in 'eight' = /eigh/ /t/).

3 The same phoneme can be represented (spelt) more than one way, as in /eɪ/ spelt as 'ay' in day, or 'a-e' as in 'take' or 'ai' as in 'snail' or 'a' as in 'baby'.

4 The same grapheme (spelling) may represent more than one phoneme, as demonstrated by the letter 'c' which may make the sound /s/ in 'city', or /c/ in 'cat'.

Children start to learn phonics focusing on the 'basic code', which refers to where a single letter makes one sound. Usually a phonics programme begins with a few consonants and short vowel phonemes, (e.g. /s/ /a/ /t/ /p/ /i/ /n/) and then moves into blending these into consonant-vowel-consonant (CVC) words (e.g. 'sat', 'tin', 'pin' etc.). Children need to begin by learning one spelling for about 40 of the approximate 44 phonemes in the English language. They then move on to the complex code which requires understanding that the phoneme can be represented by one or more letters, as in the phoneme /dʒ/ which can be represented as 'j' as in jet, or 'dge' as in badge, or 'g' as in giant or 'ge' as in barge. Details of phonemes and their common spellings can be found in a number of resources, including the National Curriculum, appendix 1 (DfE 2013) and *Letters and Sounds Notes of Guidance for Practitioners and Teachers* (DfES 2007a, b).

Pause for thought – *Checking your knowledge of the alphabetic code*

1 What is the difference between the basic and complex alphabetic code?

2 Name a word that contains a trigraph.

3 Segment the following words into their constituent phonemes:

> please
>
> school
>
> splash
>
> dear

You will find answers on page 106.

The effective teaching of phonics

It is important to bear in mind key principles that support the effective teaching of phonics. These include:

- Teaching phonics should begin with young children in Foundation Stage; however, this should be done in short and playful sessions, ensuring they are able to discriminate sounds and phonemes correctly and then it should progress quickly and aim for learning the alphabetic code between the ages of 6 and 7.

- Over-learning of phonemes that have been taught should be included in each teaching session to provide revision.

- The application of learning in reading and writing should be incorporated in every lesson.

- A multi-sensory approach should be used so that children learn from visual, auditory and kinaesthetic activities, which reinforce essential phonic knowledge and skills.

- Blending of phonemes should be explicitly taught to show how phonemes are blended, in order, from left to right, all through the word for reading.

- Segmenting should be explicitly taught to enable children to segment words into their constituent phonemes for spelling and to understand that this is the reverse of blending phonemes to read words.

- High-frequency irregular words should be taught alongside systematic phonics teaching.

- Appropriate decodable texts should be used in the early stages to support children using their phonics skills for reading, alongside ensuring a rich experience of children's books.

Assessment of progress is an important aspect with early intervention for children who are not making expected progress.

Sight vocabulary of common exception words

Skilled readers have developed a store of words they can read automatically – called a 'sight vocabulary'. In the past, this led to an emphasis on learning whole words by sight and the predominance of the 'look and say' method of teaching reading. However, it is important to realize that over-reliance on this requires good visual memory skills, which for some children presents difficulties. Children also need strategies to read unfamiliar words. Even as adults, we use phonics to read some words, for example, technical or medical words such as 'erythrocyte' (meaning red blood cell). Stuart and Stainthorp (2016: 39) note that both *lexical and phonological recoding processes operate in tandem in skilled reading*. It is therefore important for teachers to ensure that children develop a fast automatic sight vocabulary of common exception words and that teaching of such words is limited so that children at the same time learn and apply phonic skills to reading. The National Curriculum sets out a list of these words that need to be taught by different year groups (DfE 2013, appendix 1). Most early reading books said to be easily decodable using phonics also require sight-reading of some common irregular words, which are usually clearly signposted on the cover of the book.

2. Fluency – the bridge from phonics to comprehension

The development of fluency is an often neglected factor in becoming an effective reader. Studies by Aaron et al. 1999; Cutting and Scarborough 2006; and Tilstra et al. 2009 have shown that fluency improves reading comprehension. Fluency is far more than reading at speed and can be broken down into three constituent elements:

1 Accuracy (e.g. in decoding words, chunking of longer words into syllables and self-correcting).
2 Pace of reading to demonstrate automaticity.
3 *Prosody*, which is the defining feature of expressive reading. It comprises all of the variables of timing, phrasing, emphasis and intonation that speakers use to help convey aspects of meaning and to make their reading lively. This is a complex skill for young children to develop, as one of the challenges of oral reading is adding the prosodic cues that are largely absent from written language. Consider this passage from Sendak's (1992) *Where the Wild Things Are* (cited in Erekson 2010: 82).

'Now stop!' Max said and sent the wild things off to bed without *their* supper. And Max the king of all wild things was lonely and wanted to be where someone loved him best of all. [italics added]

As Erekson notes (2010: 82–3): *'When we stress the word "their" and raise its pitch, this passage highlights a previously tacit connection to a similar incident earlier in the book':*

His mother called him 'WILD THING!'
and Max said 'I'LL EAT YOU UP!'
so he was sent to bed without eating anything.

A number of strategies to help children develop these skills are discussed below.

Strategies for developing fluency

1 Ensure the book is at the right match of decodability for the child. A running record, or miscue analysis, will help assess this.

2 Increase opportunities for developing automaticity through practice at reading books that are well within a child's ability, as *'easy reading makes reading easy'*, Rasinski (n.d.).

3 Paired reading – this can be done in two ways either with another child and each reads a page and then swaps. The other way is with an adult where both read together and the adult models reading with expression, correcting the child if s/he makes an error. Periodically, they talk about the book (ensuring the child does not lose track of the story), summarizing what has happened or predicting what next.

4 Chunking or parsing reading: this requires a child to consider chunks of meaning or phrases as s/he reads. It is valuable as it breaks down a text into manageable sections and avoids putting too much strain on the working memory.

5 Repeated readings of books or passages (which could be timed) to demonstrate expression, etc.

6 After a child has had to stop and decode words, s/he is asked to reread so it sounds smooth and good to listen to.

7 Modelling fluent expressive oral reading by adults so that children see how phrased, fluent reading sounds.

8 Audio-assisted reading. Here a child reads at the same time as a text is read on tape. Research by Kuhn et al. (2006) shows that this can lead to significant gains in reading fluency.

9 Repeated reading of authentic texts for performance, such as poetry, scripts, etc.

10 Recording pupils' reading and then playing back for review with the teacher.

A useful example of teaching reading for fluency is shown in an Ofsted video of a Year 2 class during guided reading, which demonstrates the importance of re-reading for fluency. See *http://webarchive.nationalarchives.gov. uk/20130731000001/youtube.com/watch?v=wFBMYc2YuEs*

3. Developing language comprehension

Developing comprehension skills is a vital part of becoming a good reader and according to the Simple View of Reading, and all other dual language models of reading, a key factor together with word recognition. Language comprehension has received less attention than phonics and the teaching of this aspect has sometimes suffered as a result. The first thing to note is that language comprehension consists of three key aspects and should not be treated as a global construct. It includes

1 Developing vocabulary knowledge

2 Developing knowledge about language construction or syntax

3 Having knowledge about the subject and context.

Each of these aspects will be discussed in turn, together with an overview of teaching strategies.

Vocabulary

Children have widely different levels of vocabulary on entry to school and this can present difficulties in becoming readers. Word recognition is predominately seen as equating to decoding or phonics skills; however, once words are decoded they need to be within a child's lexicon. Tunmer and Chapman (2012: 457) note

> Children with poorly developed vocabulary knowledge will have trouble identifying and assigning meanings to unknown printed words (especially partially decoded words, irregularly spelled words, or words containing polyphonic or orthographically complex spelling patterns), if the corresponding spoken words are not in their listening vocabulary.

Evangelou also (2009:15) highlights the importance of vocabulary as a predictor of children's success in reading:

> Children's phonological skills are important in learning to read but so is vocabulary. Phonological skills at age 5 are better predictors of reading at the age 7 than at the age 11. Vocabulary at age 5 is a better predictor of the more complex tasks of reading at age 11 (Evangelou 2009: 15).

Biemiller (2003) demonstrates that vocabulary is largely determined by practices in the home and that this is a strong predictor of reading success. Research also shows that children from backgrounds where talking to and with children is not sufficiently valued, typically have a smaller vocabulary (White et al. 1990) and that this gap widens (Beals 1997). This can result in children from such backgrounds being trapped in a vicious circle unless specific action is taken to improve their vocabulary skills. Vadasy et al. (2015) found positive effects on vocabulary and comprehension through rich vocabulary instruction which seeks to provide depth of word knowledge through interacting with words in varying contexts, expanding word relationships and multiple word exposures.

A publication by DCSF (2008a), *Teaching Effective Vocabulary* (and still available online), provides a helpful range of methods of supporting vocabulary including the following:

- Explicit instruction on words, particularly regarding difficult words out of pupils' daily experiences

- Indirect instruction, through a rich literary environment and experience of reading materials

- Multimedia as a visual stimulus for increasing vocabulary

- Capacity methods to support development of a larger store of known words through defining word meanings; for example, a programme of encounters with new words in different ways and active processing of words and their meanings in a range of contexts

- Play with language through games, songs and jokes, alongside rich opportunities for talk, for example using 'talk partners'

Teachers also need to explicitly teach a number of new words each week which are linked to other English work; such as key words from a text being studied. Working on 'meaningful sentences' that model the use of these words in context, followed by the children creating their own sentences throughout the week, helps to ensure that the words become embedded.

Research study

A research study by Tunmer, one of the authors of the Simple View of Reading (SVR), (Tunmer and Chapman 2012), looked at whether the SVR is sufficient and whether it should be expanded to include separate components for fluency and vocabulary. Tunmer and Chapman found the following:

> Based on an examination of the available research, we concluded that neither fluency nor vocabulary needed to be incorporated into the SVR model as a separate component. Rather, the fundamental two-component structure of the model should remain intact. (Tunmer and Chapman 2012: 462)

They went on to state that although the structure of the SVR model should not be changed:

> The independent components assumption of the SVR model may need to be relaxed somewhat, as C [oral language comprehension] appears to influence R [reading comprehension] not only directly but also indirectly through D [word recognition]. (p. 464)

In other words, vocabulary affects both dimensions of the SVR – word recognition and language comprehension. This means that intervention programmes for children who are not making expected progress should focus on improving children's oral language as well as their phonics skills.

Pause for thought

- Consider how this study has implications for teaching reading.
- In what ways does vocabulary affect both word recognition and language comprehension?
- What aspects require reinforcement for struggling readers?

Syntax

As well as gaining a wide vocabulary, to gain meaning from text, pupils need to have an understanding of the components of language, or syntactic knowledge; that is the way words are ordered to form phrases, clauses and sentences. Some syntactic structures are felt to affect readers' performance, particularly verb voice (passive or active) and clause structures. Many children find sentences written in a passive form (e.g. the cat was hit by the car) rather than active form (the car hit the cat), much more difficult to understand.

Clause structures that contain a subject and a verb affect comprehension and recall. A reader finds it easier to recall independent clauses; for example, 'he used the black pen' than clauses containing a subordinating conjunction: 'before he used the black pen, he tried the blue one'. Readers also make more errors with clauses that contain a relative pronoun such as *who, which* or *that*, that are embedded in a sentence. Research by Isakson and Spyridakis (2003) shows that that text is easier for readers to understand if it contains

- Active rather than passive verb phrases
- Clauses instead of other structures such as phrases
- Independent clauses rather than dependent or relative clauses

Syntactic awareness has been shown to improve reading ability as it helps children to detect errors in their reading and self-correct. It also may support word recognition through predicting the type of word that fits in a sentence.

Semantic skills: Context/ subject matter

Developing semantic skills to be able to understand a text is predicated on skills of vocabulary and syntax as discussed. These build into understanding of longer units of language, often termed *discourse skills*. One of the first steps of developing semantic skills is ensuring knowledge about the subject or context before considering three broad skills which need to be developed: inference, comprehension monitoring and knowledge about text structure. Several studies acknowledge the influence of pre-existing knowledge of a topic on comprehension (Meyer 1984; Kintsch and van Dijk 1978; Gernsbacher et al. 1989; Kintsch et al. 1990). One of the best ways to do this before reading a book is to talk about the context and subject; to tune children in to this and to elicit their prior knowledge. If the subject matter is unfamiliar, it is necessary to introduce it, perhaps visually or with other related texts, before reading the text. It is also important to ensure that the skills of inference, comprehension monitoring and knowledge about text structure are specifically taught.

CASE STUDY: Activating prior knowledge

In one Year 4 class a teacher was introducing a new book *'The Incredible Journey'* by Sheila Burnford which tells the story of three pets as they travel over 300 miles across the Canadian wilderness searching for their owners. She began by talking about pets and children's experiences of owning pets and whether any of them had ever lost a pet. The children looked at the cover of the book and read the blurb and then working in pairs they had to come up with questions that they wanted answers to and predictions of what would happen in the story. Key questions were chosen and displayed in the classroom for discussion once they had read sections of the book. The teacher also talked about the Canadian wilderness and asked what children thought this might look like. They spent time looking at pictures, watched a short film about Canada and then imagined scenarios when they could be lost in such a place. This led to hot-seating and other role-play activities.

The children read the whole book both together as a class and independently, leading to a range of writing of their own animal stories on a similar theme.

Pause for thought

- Why do you think the teacher spent time eliciting prior knowledge of the subject of this book?
- What do you think was the impact of this?
- How might such work improve children's understanding of texts?

Inference skills

Developing skills of inference is an important aspect of understanding text. Even in relatively simple texts, inferences need to be gleaned to fully understand what is happening. Take a seemingly simple picture book such as *Rosie's Walk* by Pat Hutchins where Rosie, the hen, leaves her coop and goes for a walk. She is seemingly oblivious to the fox trying to catch her as he negotiates the various obstacles Rosie leads him through. The full story is gleaned through the complementary relationship between the words and the pictures, when the two contradict each other. There are many other examples of excellent picture books that achieve this, such as those by Anthony Browne or Colin McNaughton.

Types of inference

Inferences can be categorized into different types. Kispal's (2008) extensive literature review of the effective teaching of inference skills defines this as

> the ability to use two or more pieces of information from a text in order to arrive at a third piece of information that is implicit (Kispal 2008: 2).

Inferences are mainly text-based inferences, from information that the author supplies in the text, or knowledge-based, which rely on knowledge we have about the world to help infer things that are not explicitly stated.

Kispal (2008) cites the main categories as:

- Coherent inferences (also known as text-connecting inferences). For example: *Adam begged his mother to let him have the latest computer game.*

  The reader realizes that 'his' and 'him' in the sentence refer to Adam.

- Elaborative inferences (also known as gap-filling inferences). These elaborate on the text, for example, *John never missed an episode of Star Trek. He was a real trekky.* Here the reader would need to know that Star Trek is a science-fiction programme and that 'trekky' was an expression to describe someone that loves Star Trek.

- Local inferences are inferences that are contained in the sentence or paragraph, and require the reader to fill in the gaps.

- Global inferences help to provide a coherent picture of the whole text; the reader has to infer overarching ideas about the text.

Kispal (2008) summarizes the research into strategies to help readers to be able to draw inferences. This is helped by developing wide background knowledge and sharing, or understanding, the cultural background contained in the text. Strategies that support understanding inferences include:

- Being an active reader searching for meaning in text
- Monitoring comprehension and self-correcting errors
- Having a wide vocabulary
- Having a good working memory

Teaching strategies to help understanding inferences in text include:

- Explicit modelling by the teacher during shared or guided reading sessions
- Questioning, including generating questions
- Visualization and imagination of the text
- Summarizing what has been read
- Knowledge about text structures
- Use of cooperative group work
- Use of graphic/semantic organizers to restructure the text (see examples in Figure 5.3 below)
- Use of drama to support comprehension skills, such as hot-seating or freeze framing activities (see Güngör 2008)

A range of teaching resources to support work on inference skills can be found on websites such as TES, and Pinterest (see https://uk.pinterest.com/shortteacher/inferencing/).

You will also find useful examples and guidance on YouTube: https://www.youtube.com/watch?v=to30AJm2epQ

Developing comprehension skills is a vital part of becoming an effective reader and these skills need to be explicitly taught. As research shows, a deficit in this area has far-reaching consequences. Oakhill and Cain (2012: 92-3) note:

> Specific discourse skills that aid the ability to construct meaning from text – inference and integration, comprehension monitoring, and knowledge and use of story structure – each account for variance in concurrent measures of reading comprehension at ages 8 and 9 years, over and above vocabulary, word reading, and verbal ability.

Figure 5.3 Graphic/semantic organizers to aid comprehension of text

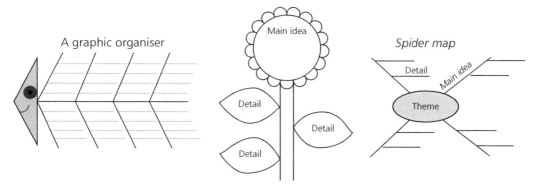

Writing

Becoming a good writer involves a range of skills. Indeed, as the writer Stephen King says '*if you want to be a good writer you must do two things above all others: read a lot and write a lot*' (2001: 164). It is not surprising that young children find writing the most challenging of aspects in learning in English: they need to develop transcription skills such as spelling, punctuation and handwriting, and understand conventions of grammar in order to accurately transfer their thoughts to the page. Research by Medwell and Wray (2007) has shown that for young children mastering the fine motor skills involved in handwriting can dominate other aspects. Together with attempting to spell words, this takes up a significant amount of working memory, leaving little room left to focus on composing text.

The National Curriculum acknowledges the complexity in becoming a good writer:

> Writing down ideas fluently depends on effective transcription: that is, on spelling quickly and accurately through knowing the relationship between sounds and letters (phonics) and understanding the morphology (word structure) and orthography (spelling structure) of words. Effective composition involves forming, articulating and communicating ideas, and then organising them coherently for a reader. This requires clarity, awareness of the audience, purpose and context, and an increasingly wide knowledge of vocabulary and grammar. Writing also depends on fluent, legible and, eventually, speedy handwriting. (DfE 2013:5)

This statement begins by focusing on the transcription skills involved in writing, and together with the two appendices on grammar, punctuation and spelling, which stipulates expectations by year groups, this can lead to a focus on transcription skills and result in children becoming demotivated. While it is very important to develop these skills, if children become reluctant writers this can have long-lasting effects. The case study below provides one example.

CASE STUDY: Writing is boring!

Lucas was six and his Year 2 class were working hard towards their SATs tests. Lucas started school loving books, but he found learning to read difficult. He struggled to grasp phonics, but with constant practice had learnt to sound out most words. He relied on this for reading and often lost the sense of what he read. When it came to writing, his class were expected to write for long periods, sometimes for a whole morning. Orally he had a great imagination and was keen to contribute, but when it came to writing, he struggled. He would take ages to get started and then when it was time to go out to play, he had to stay in and finish his work. It had become a vicious circle and he hated writing, leading to a deterioration in his behaviour in school. His teacher tried sending work home to finish or additional homework, but that just meant he switched off even more.

> ## Pause for thought
>
> - How typical do you feel this case study is?
> - What strategies could the teacher use to help Lucas?
> - How could Lucas's oral skills be better used to help him?

Refer to some of the examples of creative approaches to teaching English in chapter 3, particularly the section on the *power of play* to see how a very different approach could be used to help children like Lucas enjoy writing.

Transcription skills

While the case study has shown the dangers of an over-emphasis on skills, children clearly need to develop the ability to use phonics for reading and develop clear legible handwriting and know how to punctuate and use grammar accurately. The next section provides an overview of these skills with links to a range of resources to enable their effective teaching.

Spelling

Teaching spelling is far more than learning lists of words, which are often only remembered for a test and not applied in independent writing. As set out in *Support for Spelling* (DCSF 2009), a balanced spelling programme includes five main components:

1 Understanding the principles underpinning word construction (phonemic, morphemic and etymological)

2 Recognizing how (and how far) these principles apply to each word, in order to learn to spell words

3 Practising and assessing spelling

4 Applying spelling strategies and proofreading

5 Building pupils' self-image as spellers

English spelling is complex due to two main factors: the alphabetic code with 26 letters representing over 44 phonemes and the history of the language which has evolved from three main sources:

- Germanic – from Anglo Saxons and over half our words are derived from this

- Romance – Latin, French and influences from Spanish and Portuguese

- Greek – particularly in the areas of philosophy and physics

Based on such diverse sources, it might seem a daunting task learning to spell, yet 85 per cent of the English spelling system is predictable. One of the notable features of the patterns contained in the English written language is that the parts of words known as 'rimes' contain stable spellings and stable pronunciations. Rimes are parts of words that are spelt the same way, so that in a word such as *make* the rime is *ake* and the initial consonant or consonants are called the 'onset' of the word. The use of onset and rime, largely derived from the work of Goswami (1995), became very popular as the focus for teaching reading. While this approach has drawbacks in not teaching systematically all 44+ phonemes and their alternative spellings and pronunciations, it has real value in teaching spelling and there are 37 rimes that provide nearly 500 words in English (Wylie and Durrell 1970).

In order to spell, we need to develop two kinds of knowledge: phonemic knowledge and morphemic knowledge. A systematic phonics programme will support the development of phonemic knowledge, alongside learning spelling patterns and conventions and learning to overcome the difficulties caused by homophones (e.g. *their, there* and *they're*). What is also required is for children to understand morphology; that is the structure of words, and parts of words and their relationship to other words. *Support for Spelling* (DCSF 2009) sets out five aspects of this that require teaching:

- Root words which contain one morpheme and cannot be broken down further, such as 'friend or 'girl'
- Compound words – where two root words are combined together such as 'girlfriend'
- Suffixes added after root words that change the spelling and meaning of the word, such as walk and walked, happy and happiness
- Prefixes added before a root word which change the meaning but rarely alter the spelling, for example *mistake*
- Etymology – understanding the derivation of words, such as '*audi*' which relates to hearing and associated words such as *audible, audience, audition.* David Crystal's '*Spell It Out: The Singular Story of English Spelling*' (2012) provides a fascinating account of why there are inconsistencies such as an 'h' in 'ghost' but not in 'goat'. An amusing and brief animation showing the History of English could also be useful to introduce this to children: https://www.youtube.com/watch?v=H3r9bOkYW9s&feature=share.
- Studying etymology encourages children to explore our language and classroom strategies as a spelling. 'Wonder Wall' can be used for children to ask spelling questions that are puzzling them, such as '*what has 'secret' got to do with being a 'secretary*'?

A helpful teaching sequence for spelling is set out in *Support for Spelling* (DCSF 2009: 10). See Figure 5.4 for details.

One commonly used strategy for learning spellings is to learn spelling rules. However as Gentry (1987) and McGuinness (2004) have argued, there are so many exceptions that they are rarely useful. For example, the commonly known rule 'i' before 'e' except after 'c', often does not work (as in 'seeing', 'weigh' and 'their'). This

Figure 5.4 The teaching sequence for spelling. DCSF (2009)
Source: webarchive.nationalarchives.gov.uk/20110809091832/...org.uk/collection/35326

THE TEACHING SEQUENCE

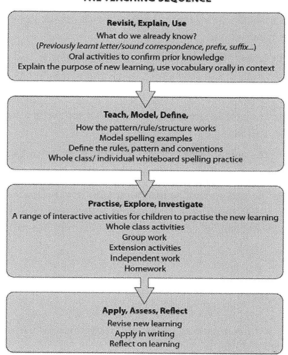

"rule" is probably well known because it rhymes, rather than because it is particularly useful. Nevertheless, there are some general principles that are worth examining with children, for example: for making words ending with 'y' plural, if a vowel precedes the 'y', add an 's'; if a consonant precedes the 'y', remove the 'y' and add 'ies'. One approach that helps in teaching spelling is to adopt an investigative approach, where children look at lots of examples and work out the principle themselves. *Support for Spelling* (DCSF 2009) provides many examples of investigations for different year groups. Appendix 1 of the National Curriculum (pages 50–74) sets out lists of words to be learnt by year groups but also emphasizes that phonic knowledge will help underpin spelling and that *pupils also need to understand the role of morphology and etymology* (DfE 2013: 50).

Handwriting

The National Curriculum states that writing *'depends on fluent, legible and, eventually, speedy handwriting'* (2013: 16). The Curriculum provides statutory guidance by year groups on the development and teaching of handwriting.

Brien (2012: 109) maintains that children need to learn to start a letter at the right point and know the first movement; this will help ensure that correct formation will follow. Principles of letter formation include:

- Clockwise and anti-clockwise movements – making the right movement is essential in handwriting
- Many of our letters start with an anti-clockwise curve: a, c, d, e, f, g, o, q, s
- Another important group start with a downstroke: b, h, i, j, k, l, m, n, p, r, t, u, y (in most styles)
- The other lower-case letters are the ones which start with a slanting downstroke: v, w, x
- z doesn't fit into any of these groups, and both e and s are slight anomalies

Medwell and Wray's research (2007), as cited earlier, emphasizes the importance of developing legible and speedy handwriting and '*in particular the automaticity of letter production*' as this '*frees up working memory to deal with the complex tasks of planning, organizing, revising and regulating the production of text*' (2007: 11–12).

Punctuation

Punctuation has two main aspects: rules and conventions. Conventions are more open to interpretation. Rules include:

- All sentences begin with capital letters.
- Sentences must end with full stops, question marks or exclamation marks.
- Apostrophes are used to show elision (can't, wouldn't etc.) and to show possession (Alfie's, Manuel's etc.).

There is also a degree of flexibility and choice in the use of punctuation. Writers may choose to use punctuation marks in different ways. For example, some people use far more exclamation marks than others, while others include more commas in their writing. The National Curriculum (DfE 2013: 67–9) provides a list of what punctuation should be taught and in which years, together with a glossary of terms.

Teaching punctuation can be done in interesting investigative ways. Finding examples of punctuation that alter the meaning of a sentence can be an engaging activity, such as:

A sign that said: *'Slow children at play'*
which could have read:
'Slow, children at play.'

Or

A piece of dialogue from a child's story:
Shall we eat Grandma?
which, one would hope, should have read:
Shall we eat, Grandma?

You will find a range of useful teaching approaches in Waugh et al. (2016) and for 20 useful strategies, see https://www.teachit.co.uk/attachments/22889/20-teaching-ideas-for-punctuation.pdf. *For teaching punctuation using comics,* see www.storyboardthat.com/articles/e/punctuation

Other useful websites include
http://www.teachingideas.co.uk/subjects/punctuation
https://uk.pinterest.com/explore/teaching-punctuation/

Grammar

'Grammar is the study of how we make sense in speaking or writing so that we can understand people who speak the same language as we do. It's no more mysterious than that' (Reedy and Bearne 2013: 5). They also state:

Good writing is what works to do the job the writer wants. And studying how language works – grammar – should help young writers to say what they want to say as effectively as they can. (2013: 4)

The National Curriculum requires that pupils should

write clearly, accurately and coherently, adapting their language and style in and for a range of contexts, purposes and audiences. (2013: 14)

The Curriculum sets out in a statutory appendix the expectations for teaching grammar, and this is assessed by a statutory test introduced in 2013 in England. This has presented a challenge for teachers, many of whom were not taught grammar explicitly and found this daunting.

It is important to realize that there is a difference between implicit and explicit knowledge of grammar. Most children start school knowing many rules of spoken language, but this is implicit. Most adults, who profess to not know much about grammar, actually do and use it effectively. What they don't know is some of the terminology, so that being asked to define a 'modal verb' sends them into a panic. However, there are numerous resources to help teachers become more familiar with this terminology, not least the appendix and glossary in the National Curriculum.

Teaching grammar does not mean a focus on decontextualized exercises which can be tedious; instead it can involve learning about language in playful ways such as with jokes, rhymes and investigations to help children develop a genuine interest in language. Exploring grammar can be done in a number of ways, such as the use of good quality literature. Reedy and Bearne (2013: 7) set out a sequence for teaching grammar, called REDM as set out below:

↓   Reading and investigation
↓   Explicit teaching
↓   Discussion and experimentation
↓   Making controlled writing choices

Read the case study below which uses this teaching sequence.

CASE STUDY: The REDM sequence for teaching grammar

Kennedy (2014) cites the example of an academy in Birmingham where the teachers have used the REDM model since the introduction of the statutory test. In Year 2 the teacher based a unit of work around the text Jan and Jerry Oke's *Naughty Bus* (2004). The theme was toys and the children had many opportunities to write, describing favourite toys, wrote poems non-chronological reports and gave their views on the text. The classroom had a huge red bus displayed with windows representing each 'mini adventure' of the main character. In this context, the children looked at word classes to develop the use of effective verbs and noun phrases to describe the characters. Explicit teaching of grammar was integrated into the teaching sequence, modelled by the teacher. For example, they selected adjectives to describe the bus using a zone of relevance chart and selected appropriate adjectives from those printed on cards. Following shared writing, children wrote a paragraph describing the character using the adjectives in differentiated and supported ways. An independent writing area in the class provided opportunities for children to choose to write about the book or theme. In order to make controlled choices, the children went on a bus ride with clipboards and digital cameras. Back in the classroom they collected their ideas and photographs. Using oral rehearsal these were shaped into lines for their list poems. Because of their experience of developing noun phrases, they were more confident in making language choices. Lines from the poems included:

A big brown bag stuffed with clothes
Big smiling baby in a pushchair
Old man reading his book
A lovely baby crying
A big blue bag full of food and vegetables
A little child sleeping in the bus
(cited in Kennedy 2014: 3)

Children's final writing outcomes: 'a Naughty Bus adventure', demonstrated that they were applying what they had learnt.

> ## Pause for thought
>
> - In what ways did the exploration of the book form the basis of this teaching sequence?
> - How was grammar explicitly taught in this example?
> - How did first-hand experience support the quality of writing?

What this case study and other research, such as a large-scale study by Myhill et al. (2012), show is that there are significant positive effects from teaching grammar in the context of teaching about writing.

Research study

A study by Safford (2016) has examined the impact of the grammar element of the statutory test in spelling, punctuation and grammar and found that:

1 *Since the introduction of the statutory SPaG test in primary schools, time spent teaching decontextualized and contextualized grammar has increased significantly.*

2 *Grammar is now taught explicitly and formally as a classroom literacy routine.*

3 *The test format influence grammar teaching content and approaches.*

4 *Teachers observe that pupils enjoy learning grammar and taking the test.*

5 *Teachers disagree about the extent to which explicit grammar teaching and testing have a positive impact on pupils' language and literacy skills.*

6 *Teachers feel more confident about teaching grammar.*

> ## Pause for thought
>
> - What are some of the benefits of a greater focus on grammar?
> - What are some of the challenges for teachers?
> - How have pupils reacted in this research study?

Composition skills

This chapter has focused on teaching the skills of English in contextualized ways. A number of examples of creative approaches to teaching English have been explored in Chapter 3, illustrating the value of integrating the four modes of language. One well-known approach to teaching writing is 'Talk for Writing'. This approach developed for the National Strategies (DCSF 2008b) by Pie Corbett, embodies talk in every stage of the teaching sequence for writing (see figure 5.5). This process involves the learning and repeating of oral stories, as rehearsal for writing. The sequence starts with imitation of stories, then moves to innovation, where stories are adapted and finally invention where new stories are created. Pie Corbett has developed an extensive range of resources to support this (see www.talk4writing.co.uk). You can also watch Pie modelling shared writing with teachers at http://youtu.be/LGMv6Tf-Lm4.

The National Curriculum also states that children need to write clearly, accurately and coherently, and adapt their language and style 'for a range of contexts, purposes and audiences' (DfE 2013: 5). Having an authentic purpose and real audience can have a profound impact on children's writing (see Chapter 3 and the case study 'The Promise' for a powerful example). Schools find that competitions such as the BBC 500 Words (http://bbc.in/2gQezUY) can be a powerful stimulus. Blogging is another form of writing that provides an instant audience; Make Waves (www.makewav.es)

Figure 5.5 The teaching sequence for writing (PNS/UKLA 2004: 7)

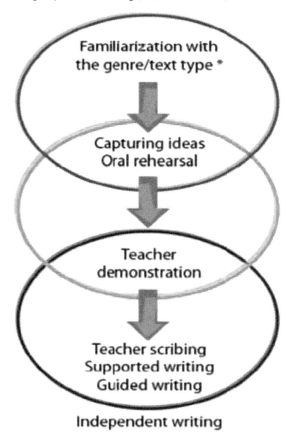

Familiarization with
the genre/text type *

Capturing ideas
Oral rehearsal

Teacher
demonstration

Teacher scribing
Supported writing
Guided writing

Independent writing

is a safe learning platform for children where they can upload written articles, audio or video to share with other children.

In Chapter 6 you will find extensive guidance on teaching approaches for writing.

Summary

This chapter has been wide-ranging, examining the skills required to master speaking and listening, reading and writing. It has emphasized the centrality of talk to developing proficiency in reading and writing and provided detailed examples of teaching strategies to support this. While a full range of skills has been examined across all modes of language, the chapter has highlighted those that have suffered from a lack of attention. So that in teaching reading the dominant focus on phonics often insufficiently ensures the development of skills of fluency and comprehension. Teaching of transcription skills of spelling, handwriting and punctuation, alongside the conventions of grammar have also been explored; emphasizing the importance of teaching these explicitly and in contextualized ways. What teaching of skills must not do, as in the case study of Lucas, is to lead to demotivating pupils. In contrast, another case study, the REDM sequence for teaching grammar, demonstrates powerfully how explicit teaching of skills can be done using literature and first-hand experience as a stimulus. In this way, boys such as Lucas can be active and engaged.

From reading this chapter you will have developed your knowledge and understanding of

- The skills involved in becoming proficient speakers, listeners, readers and writers
- The elements of vocabulary, spelling, grammar and punctuation and how to teach these in creative ways
- Research into developing the skills in learning in English
- Case studies of schools that are explicitly teaching the skills to exemplify developing mastery in contextualized ways

Recommended reading

For speaking and listening:

Allott, K. and Waugh, D. (2016). *Language and Communication in Primary Schools.* London: Sage.

Jolliffe, W. (2007). *Cooperative Learning in the Classroom: Putting it in Practice.* London: Sage.

Jones, D. and Hodson, P. (2012). *Unlocking Speaking and Listening*, 2nd ed. London: Routledge.

First Steps (2013). *Speaking and Listening Map of Development*, Department of Education Western Australia.
Available from http://det.wa.edu.au/stepsresources/detcms/navigation/first-steps-literacy/

For reading:

Stuart, M. and Stainthorp, R. (2016). *Reading Development and Teaching*. London: Sage.
Waugh, D. and Neaum, S. *Beyond Early Reading*. Northwich: Critical Publishing.
Jolliffe, W. and Waugh, D. with Carss, A. (2015). *Teaching Systematic Synthetic Phonics in Primary Schools*, 2nd ed. London: Learning Matters SAGE.

For writing:

Waugh, D., Warner C. and Waugh R. (2016). *Teaching Grammar, Punctuation and Spelling in Primary Schools*, 2nd ed. London: Sage.
Reedy, D. and Bearne, E. (2013). *Teaching Grammar Effectively in Primary Schools*. UKLA.
Waugh, D., Allott, K., Waugh, R., English, E. and Bulmer, E. (2014). *The Spelling, Punctuation and Grammar App*. Morecambe: Children Count Ltd (available through the App Store).

Answers to pause for thought

Checking your knowledge of the alphabetic code

1 The difference between the basic and complex alphabetic code is that the basic code involves being able to make simple correspondences between single letters which make a single sound and learn one spelling for about forty phonemes. The complex code requires understanding that a phoneme can be represented by one or more letters; the same phoneme can be spelt more than one way and the same spelling may represent more than one phoneme.

2 Words that contain a trigraph include l**igh**t, **h**air or ca**tch**

3 Segment the following words into their constituent phonemes:

> please – /p/ /l/ ea/ /se/
> school – /s/ /ch/ /oo/ /l/
> splash – /s/ /p/ /l/ /a/ /sh/
> dear – /d/ /ear/

Chapter 6
Children's Ideas:
Engaging Children with Writing

Chapter objectives

By reading this chapter you will develop your understanding of the following:

- Different approaches to teaching and learning writing and how these can be used to engage children with writing
- Pupil performance in writing and gender differences
- How grammar can be taught through writing
- Modelling writing for children
- Ways in which teachers can write with and for children

Introduction

This chapter first explores different approaches to writing and examines strategies which teachers and children can use to plan and develop writing. There is an emphasis upon the role of the teacher, both in modelling writing and acting as a scribe who discusses the writing process and in writing with and for children. The chapter goes on to show how grammar can be taught and learnt through writing, and stresses the importance of providing a varied diet of writing for children. Research and data on children's writing are also presented and discussed. This chapter should be looked at in conjunction with Chapter 3 on promoting creativity in English, since many of the strategies discussed there are ideal stimuli for writing. The focus in this chapter is on strategies, but before any strategies can be deployed, it is important that children feel they have something they want to write about.

Teaching approaches for writing

The principal approaches to teaching writing are modelled writing, shared writing, supported composition and guided writing. It is helpful to think of these as stages in the scaffolding of writing support, so that children observe a model of good writing, take part in writing together in shared writing, and in supported composition, the teacher and class experiment together, trying out words, sentences and language structure. In guided writing, the scaffolding is the teacher supporting children to write, working in a group to focus on an aspect of writing, followed by children writing independently.

These stages may not all be necessary in producing a piece of writing and teachers need to select what is an appropriate level of support for the children they are working with. One of the reoccurring issues is that teachers themselves lack confidence in writing, leading to issues with modelling it. Cremin and Baker (2010) argued that to improve the teaching of writing, teachers need to be writers themselves and they need real opportunities to write at their own level and reflect upon the process. Ofsted (2009a, b) also found that teachers who were confident as writers taught writing effectively.

Quigley (2013) provides some very useful tips for effective shared and guided writing to support mastery:

1 Have a clear idea of what the desired 'mastery model' is, including having some elements prepared in advance, such as specific vocabulary, or sentence structure.

2 If teachers find that pupils do not stay on task during shared writing, selecting a pupil to scribe can help and allows the teacher to manage the room.

3 Being very clear about expectations and how pupils will contribute, such as raising their hands first.

4 Pre-plan questions in advance which can be highly specific and differentiated. Consider how 'open' or 'closed' each question should be.

5 'Pose, pause and bounce' questions around the room. The bouncing is important as it keeps the class focused as they know anyone can be questioned at any time.

6 During guided writing it is important to ensure everyone is writing simultaneously.

7 Circulate the room and praise efforts with specific feedback and invite critical challenges and revisions.

8 Consider how ongoing feedback can be given, such as the ABC feedback model, where A = add to the writing, B = build upon the writing and C = challenge what has been written.

9 Ensure pupils review the writing comparing with the 'default' model and reflect on what they have learnt about writing.

Research study

The *Transforming Writing Project* (Rooke 2013) was a two-year action research project, which developed a model for the teaching and learning of writing to fully incorporate a focus on embedded formative assessment. Twelve schools took part in the first year and ten schools developed a model for training other teachers in their school and visited other schools. The project incorporated professional development for teachers on *Talk for Writing* led by Pie Corbett and Julia Strong and included sessions on formative assessment informed by the work of Wiliam (2011a,b) and Clarke (2014). Further workshops centred on using formative assessment in the construction of toolkits (writing goals); using formative assessment to help children internalize patterns they need to make progress; using formative assessment in shared and guided writing and using formative assessment in marking and oral feedback.

Sixty-eight per cent of children in the study made more than expected progress in writing in a year and this applied to both boys and girls. The project also impacted positively on children's attitudes to writing. Teachers used a wide range of strategies to develop children's independent use of formative assessment using a structured model of writing that facilitated children's guided experimentation with talk about their own and each other's writing. Extended collaborative talk about the genre of writing before children start writing provides a rich resource for children to revisit and from which to draw during all stages of their writing. The project cites twelve classroom approaches that impacted on children's writing (Rooke 2013: 13):

1 *Teachers used a variety of marking techniques to engage children in assessment.*

2 *Teachers and children collaboratively constructed writing goals to guide assessment.*

3 *Teachers collected and displayed knowledge about writing for children to use for assessment.*

4 *Teachers created dialogic spaces for children to collaboratively talk about and assess their writing.*

5 *Teachers modelled how writers talk and think when assessing their own writing.*

6 *Teachers found that shared reading comprehension and children's assessment of their own writing were mutually supportive.*

7 *Teachers created safe learning environments for children to collaboratively assess their own writing.*

8 *Teachers had a clear sense of how children's assessment talk about writing should progress.*

9 *Teachers used flexible and responsive planning.*

10 *Teachers used mini writing lessons to rapidly respond to formative assessment.*

11 *Teachers used guided writing lessons to rapidly respond to formative assessment.*

12 *Teachers' confidence and credibility supported children's formative assessment of writing.*

Pause for thought

- Consider how important the relationship in this project was between teaching writing with a focus on talk, and the use of formative assessment.
- Does the need for extensive professional development provided in this project indicate that this is an area where teachers lack confidence?
- How important were the opportunities for pupils to collaboratively assess their writing?

CASE STUDY: Developing the pedagogy for shared writing

Stephen, a student teacher, had been asked to use shared writing to model story openings. He planned for this by writing his own story opening and then using it in his lesson. As he wrote on the board and the children watched, he carefully copied out his writing and then asked the children about it. *What did they like? What could be improved? Had he made any mistakes?* Children then began to write their own story openings.

Throughout the shared writing, children had been attentive and quiet, with only a few responding to Stephen's questions.

When his class teacher debriefed him after the lesson, she praised him for his careful preparation, but asked him why he had copied his writing rather than preparing some ideas and thinking about possible phrasing and vocabulary and then creating the writing as he wrote, drawing upon the children's ideas. Stephen said that he did not feel sufficiently confident about class management or his own writing ability to do this, but the teacher looked at his writing and told him that he should feel confident, given the quality of what he had written. She offered to take the next writing lesson and asked Stephen to observe her doing shared writing and said that she would welcome his feedback.

Stephen noticed that the experienced teacher's lesson included much more interaction with children than his and that children were very engaged and eager to contribute suggestions for both plot and phrasing. There were lots of opportunities for children to 'think-pair-share' so that they could discuss their ideas and tell other children and the teacher about them. Stephen also noticed that the teacher thought aloud as she constructed sentences, and frequently changed words or invited suggestions. He felt he understood the potential of shared writing much better, but was still slightly nervous about managing a class and about his own writing, so the teacher suggested the team teach shared writing in the next lesson and said that she would intervene whenever he wanted her to. They decided upon a prearranged signal which Stephen could use when he wanted her to take over.

The ensuing lesson was very successful and Stephen actually only handed over to the teacher on three occasions. In subsequent lessons he grew in confidence and actually formed a writing club which met at lunchtimes during the last three weeks of his placement.

Pause for thought

- How confident do you feel about modelling writing?
- What could you do to prepare for shared writing?
- Inevitably, if you invite children's contributions and ask them to discuss ideas in pairs, your class may be noisy. What strategies could you use to draw them together and retain an orderly atmosphere?
- If you are worried about making mistakes when you do shared writing, how could you use this to make teaching points?

Shared writing

Shared writing involves more than simply writing as children observe. It provides opportunities to model the thought processes which writers go through as they compose. It 'scaffolds' the transcriptional aspects of writing, as well as showing that there are many ways in which sentences can be constructed and enabling discussion about vocabulary usage. Links can be made to reading and examples can be explored as the teacher and the class strive to produce engaging writing. When modelling in this way, teachers should make repeated reference to the genre and intended audience for the writing and invite suggestions for how the writing can be made appropriate.

Through shared writing, teachers can 'scaffold' children's subsequent writing, for example by using subheadings for non-fiction work, or a range of paragraph openers (first, next, finally etc), which children can then build their writing around.

Shared writing can evolve during a lesson, so that the teacher might initially *demonstrate* writing by scribing her own words while thinking aloud about vocabulary and phrasing choices for a couple of sentences. This can then develop as children make suggestions which the teacher scribes and discusses, perhaps inviting groups to suggest the next sentence or adjectives to describe a character. This can be followed by *supported composition* in which children write, perhaps using tablets or mini whiteboards, before sharing their ideas, some of which can be discussed and incorporated into a whole-class composition. All of this might be described as a gradual reduction in teacher support leading to pupils taking increased responsibility for their writing (see Graham et al. 2012, 2016).

Strategies for writing

There are key elements in a writing process which can be modelled by teachers so that children become familiar with them and confident about using them:

Planning – setting goals and generating ideas before pupils begin writing. Students should write down goals so that they can refer back to them as they write. Example strategies include goal setting, activating prior knowledge, graphic organizers, discussion.

Drafting – focusing on getting down key ideas. Pupils should set their writing out in a logical order. Although accurate spelling, grammar and handwriting are important, at this stage they are not the main focus. Example strategies: making lists, graphic organizers, writing frames (see Nick's planning below).

Sharing – sharing ideas or drafts throughout the writing process gives pupils feedback. Example strategies: in pairs, listen and read along as the author reads aloud.

Evaluating – checking that the writing goals are being achieved throughout the process. This can be done by pupils as they re-read their writing or through feedback

Figure 6.1 Alex's planning and drafting for writing about senses

from adults or peers. Example strategies: self-monitoring and evaluation by asking questions like, 'have I met my goals?' and 'have I used appropriate vocabulary?'

Revising – making changes to content of writing in light of feedback and self-evaluation. Where digital media are available, this can be done easily and quickly. With pen and paper, it should be accepted that work may become messy but that at this stage the audience will be limited. Example strategies: peers placing a question mark next to things they do not understand and pupils thinking of synonyms for repeated words.

Editing – making changes to ensure the text is accurate and coherent. At this stage, spelling and grammar assume greater importance and pupils will need to recognize that their work will need to be accurate if readers are to engage with it and extract the intended information from it. Example strategies: checking capital letters and full stops and reviewing spellings using a dictionary.

Publishing – presenting the work so that others can read it. This may not be the outcome for all pieces of writing, but when used appropriately it can provide a strong incentive for pupils to produce high-quality writing and encourage them to carefully revise and edit in particular. Example strategies: displaying work, presenting to other classes, sending copies to parents and carers.

It is important to use these strategies judiciously. Not all writing needs to be drafted, so children need to understand when it is appropriate to use the strategies and when a first attempt is sufficient. For example, notes, texts, informal letters and lists may require little revision, whereas a poem, story, formal letter or a piece of non-fiction writing which is to be displayed or presented to others requires accuracy and needs to be honed and refined until it is 'publishable'.

Figure 6.2 A vocabulary display for children to use when writing

Research: Pupils' progress in writing in England

In 2012, the Department for Education produced an analysis of the evidence about pupils' performance in writing in England (DfE 2012).

- Writing is the subject with the worst performance compared with reading, maths and science at Key Stages 1 and 2.
- There is a consistent gender gap in pupils' performance in writing with girls outperforming boys throughout all Key Stages.
- At the Foundation Stage 71 per cent of children were working securely within the early learning goals of the Communication, Language and Literacy learning area.
- At Key Stage 1, 83 per cent of children achieved the expected level national teacher assessments in writing; at Key Stage 2, 81 per cent of pupils achieved the expected level.
- At GCSE only 69 per cent of pupils achieved a grade A*-C in English.

It should be noted that the 2016 Key Stage 2 SATs, which were acknowledged to be more challenging than previously and therefore 'not comparable to those for earlier years' (DfE 2016a, b: 1), showed that 74 per cent of children achieved the expected standard in writing compared with 66 per cent in reading, perhaps indicating that schools are addressing the problem (see Chapter 7 for details of changes). However, writing alone was teacher assessed, while reading, grammar, punctuation and spelling, and mathematics were tested by means of external tests.

Implications of findings

Higgins' (2015) analysis of the above data and other research leads him to conclude that we need

- Explicit teaching of the *process* of writing and strategies which emphasize the different stages, such as planning, drafting and sharing ideas
- Emphasis on self-evaluation and developing pupils' capability to assess their own work through revising and editing
- Work on summarizing texts in writing (such as through précis) and combining sentences
- Modelling of specific skills to support pupils, but where the support is deliberately faded out so that there is a gradual shift in responsibility from the teacher to the pupil so that they become independent writers

- Engaging pre-writing activities which help them to develop a range of strategies: this could be by helping them work out what they already know, or to research an unfamiliar topic, or arrange their ideas visually or thematically

(Higgins, 2015)

This accords with studies which show the value of shared writing, since it models the process of writing, and it also sits well with the studies which have identified strategies for writing (see above).

A gender gap

In 2016, the gap between boys and girls achieving the expected grade was higher for writing than for any other subject (81 per cent of girls achieved the grade in writing compared with 68 per cent of boys).

The gender gap exists internationally in literacy, with the 2011 Progress in International Reading Literacy Study (PIRLS) showing that in forty of the forty-five countries participating, girls outperformed boys in reading. For writing, it has been argued that boys' fine motor skills are weaker than girls (Daly 2003; DfES 2007a, b; Goddard 2009) and that this leads to frustration when they come to handwrite.

According to Clark (2013), boys are much more likely to state that they do not enjoy writing (20.9 per cent compared with 8.6 per cent for girls). We should also consider how the gap between boys and girls might be addressed. Daly (2003) has argued that boys should be given more freedom to choose what they write about, while Bhojwani (2015) suggests that boys can be motivated by multimodal texts which include sound, writing, image and movement. A project developed by the United Kingdom Literacy Association (UKLA 2004) to raise boys' engagement, motivation and achievements in writing, using either **visual stimuli** including integrated technologies **drama** and other speaking and listening activities, showed that these approaches had significant benefits:

The combination of an extended approach to teaching which required specific attention to drama and/or visual approaches has proved highly successful in raising boys' achievements in writing. There have been significant gains in terms of professional development and the establishment of a strong core of local expertise. Although the focus was on underachieving boys, the work has also had beneficial effects on the rest of the pupils' writing and attitudes to themselves as writers. (UKLA 2004: 45)

It seems clear that there continues to be a gender gap in writing performance and it is important to take this into account when planning writing activities. However, some of the strategies which can develop boys' writing may also benefit girls.

Pause for thought

- What is your experience of differences between boys and girls in attitudes to and performance in writing?
- Have you observed any strategies which teachers have deployed to engage boys with writing?

Different text genres

We have looked at the process of writing and ways in which teachers can model and scaffold for children. We now turn to what might be written. The National Curriculum for England (DfE 2013: 10) does not give the same attention to experience a range of genres as its predecessors or the Literacy Framework (DfEE 1998). However, it does state:

> The writing they do should include narratives, explanations, descriptions, comparisons, summaries and evaluations: such writing supports them in rehearsing, understanding and consolidating what they have heard or read.

Pause for thought

Look at the writing produced by Elizabeth in Year 4 with a trainee teacher, Raam. It is an example of non-fiction writing, but it is personalized and creative. In which of the above categories would you place it?

Research: A variety of forms

Based upon a meta-analysis of research, Higgins (2015) concluded:

- Evidence (Graham et al. 2012) indicates it is important to expose pupils to a *variety of forms of writing* and to practise these so that they learn to write for a variety of purposes and master different genres of writing (e.g. description, narration, persuasion or argumentation, information and explanatory texts).
- Seeing examples of good writing in these different forms and being given positive feedback when they develop key features is essential.
- Teach explicit strategies. For example, in descriptive writing one approach which has been shown to be effective is to link written descriptions with the senses: *What did you see? How did it look? What sounds did you hear? What did you touch? How did it feel? What could you smell? What did you taste?*

Figure 6.3 Writing produced by Elizabeth and Raam, a trainee teacher

JASPER, MY CRAZY DOG!

My crazy springer spaniel, Jasper, is a black and white dog who looks big for two years old. Occasionally, he is very fury however sometimes he gets really dirty. I can often feel rough patches behind his dark, black ears. He gets muddy really quickly and needs a bath at least five times a month. When Jasper wants food, he pulls a sad face and his big, beautiful hazel eyes shine like the sun.

FUN FACTS ABOUT JASPER:

❖ He is very clumsy as he once fell into a long, cold lake.
❖ When he has a bath, he tries to jump out and run around my house.
❖ He always tries to get the white carpet dirty.
❖ Jasper supports Sunderland football team.
❖ My crazy dog eats everything except for jacket potatoes because they make him vomit.
❖ He loves to play anywhere and everywhere and his best friend is Lorna's dog, Smudge.

Pause for thought

If we are to enable children to experience a variety of genres, we need to be familiar with them ourselves. Look at the list below and decide which forms you feel confident you both know and could teach.

narrative prose	blogs	magazines	cartoons
non-fiction books	advertisements	comics	comics
web story books	songs	menus	timetables
web pages	newspapers	leaflets	newspaper articles
web logs	catalogues	posters	pop-up and lift the flap books
picture books	poetry	texting	
instructions	texts	sports reports	emails
letters (formal and informal)			

Making collections

A good way to develop a knowledge of a range of genres and provide a useful resource bank is to make collections of a range of texts. These can be displayed on walls of, in albums or PowerPoint presentations, so that children can become familiar with them. Look carefully at the features of the texts: what style are they written in? What kind of vocabulary is used? How are they set out? Besides collecting examples of the texts above, having a selection of excerpts from texts can be invaluable when introducing writing activities. The following will be helpful:

Story openings

Examples can be taken from well-known children's stories, with the books displayed next to a wall display of story openings. These can be discussed in shared reading and children can offer opinions as to which are effective in making them want to read on.

Descriptions of characters and settings

Not only can these provide examples for children's own writing, but they can be a resource for discussing adjectives, adverbs, synonyms, similes, metaphors and other descriptive devices.

Descriptions of exciting events

These can offer an opportunity to consider how a range of verbs might be used to create tension. They might also stimulate drama activities prior to writing.

Interesting dialogue

Interesting use of a range of verbs as alternatives to *said* might be discussed. There may also be examples of dialect and even accent where an author presents some words in such a way that the reader can tell how they were pronounced. Good examples can be found in Frances Hodgson Burnett's *The Secret Garden* and Roald Dahl's *Danny the Champion of the World.*

Picture books (see also Chapter 3 on Creativity)

Many picture books can be enjoyed by younger children and studied at a more advanced level by older children. Lane (1980) identified three key functions of illustrations in books and each has a place in the classroom. We might collect examples of books where the pictures are *graphics decoration*, in that they add little to the meaning of the text but make it more attractive and interesting for the reader. Books which provide *narrative illustration* use pictures to mirror the text, while *interpretative illustrations* add another layer of meaning or a richness of meaning to the text, for example, Anthony Browne's *The Tunnel.*

There are also excellent examples of wordless texts for older children which promote thinking and discussion and which could be a stimulus for writing. For example, *The Arrival* by Shaun Tan (2007) tells the story of an immigrant arriving on Ellis Island in the United States. Harris Burdick's strange and mysterious pictures can be found online (http://www.powershow.com/view4/46cb9a-MzBhN/The_Mysteries_of_Harris_Burdick_By_Chris_Van_Allsburg_powerpoint_ppt_presentation) and always arouse interest and discussion. They also make excellent starting points for creative writing.

It may be that after looking at examples of picture books children could use pictures as a starting point for writing rather than as something to be created as a sort of reward for completing their writing. For younger children and those who struggle with writing, this may be a good way of enabling them to tell a story. Kress (1997) looked at how children symbolically represent what they know before they can write it down. He maintained that before children begin to write they use a range of symbolic ways to represent what they know, can do and are thinking.

Varieties of non-fiction

These might include reference texts such as dictionaries, encyclopaedias and thesauruses, as well as catalogues and text books about a range of subjects, timetables, maps, listings of TV programmes, league tables and music charts. Examples of web pages in a variety of forms can be shown as part of shared reading.

The English National Curriculum does not provide details of different non-fiction genres to be studied in the way that previous curricula did: that *the writing children do should include narratives, explanations, descriptions, comparisons, summaries and evaluations* (DfE 2013: 6.3). This does not mean that other types of texts should not be part of children's writing diet and it is important that this includes a range of forms of communication, including digital and multimodal texts. As Warner (2017: 188) argues, if such texts are not experienced in school, 'The gap between cultural practices at home and at school will widen as technology advances'.

In engaging children with any text, it is important to make use of modelling, as discussed earlier, so that children see the characteristics of different genres and styles of writing. In the next section, an approach which involves modelling and writing with children is explored. You will find examples of writing which have been produced as a result of cooperative work between trainee teachers and children,

Figure 6.4 Writing by Lucas in Year 4 and Veronica, a trainee teacher

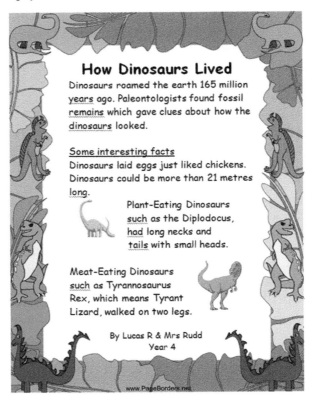

including the one below in which the trainee teacher and Lucas discussed dinosaurs, prepared for researching and writing about dinosaurs by agreeing to find information and bring it to school, and then wrote about them in Lucas's words, which were subsequently typed and presented by the trainee.

Writing with and for children

Besides modelling writing through shared writing, teachers might consider writing for children as well as with them. This could take the form of a story opening which the class continue either collectively or in groups or individually. It could be a short poem such as a haiku, cinquain, tankas, limerick or triolet, or a piece of non-fiction text. Examples of playscripts and dialogue can be written and then performed by children before they continue them by adding further dialogue. Roth and Guinee (2011) describe how teachers can work with children using interactive *writing* 'to construct a meaningful text while discussing the details of the writing process' (p. 333).

Why write for children?

- It shows you value writing
- It helps you to understand the challenges children face
- It gives you the opportunity to see how an audience responds to writing
- It provides a model for children's writing
- You can target children's interests and even include them in a story

Figure 6.5 Shark fact file produced by Oliver and Gemma, a trainee teacher

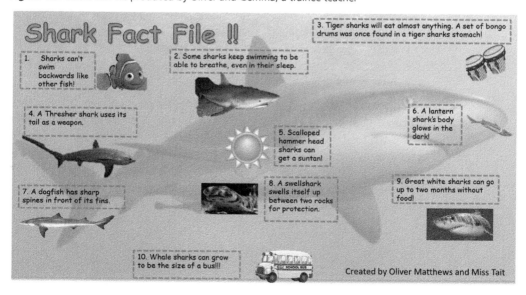

Research focus: Teachers as writers

Cremin and Baker (2014) maintained:

> In taking a more consciously reflective role as writers, teachers often feel impelled to make changes to their pedagogy and practice and this can shape the children's views of their teachers as writers and their growing competence and confidence as young writers themselves (Bearne et al. 2011). A stronger community of writers can be built in the classroom if teachers and support staff are able to connect to and share their writing lives and enable children to recognise and celebrate the diversity of their own writing practices. (p. 5)

A 15-month-long action research programme, *Writing is Primary*, instigated and funded by the Esmée Fairbairn Foundation, and run in groups of schools in Bury, Kent/Medway, and Worcester over the school year 2007/08 concluded:

> Those who enjoy writing for themselves, who have confidence in their writing skills and who are able to share all this with their pupils seem, by most accounts, more likely to teach writing effectively than those who lack this experience. (Ings 2010: 75)

CASE STUDY: A novel written by 46 people

Teachers might write to provide examples for children, but their writing could be taken a step further if children become engaged with what they write and then contribute to the development of a substantial piece which can ultimately be shared more widely. The book cover below belongs to a novel, *The Wishroom* (Waugh et al. 2017), written and illustrated with 45 children from 15 primary schools in East Durham. In this case, the story opening set up situations for children to dramatize and write about. It evolved week by week as children's writing was weaved into the plot. There were opportunities for shared writing and for children to read the story as it developed before planning their next contribution.

The writing had to be structured and discussions led to the plot evolving and changing. The final draft comprised more than 36,000 words, the overwhelming majority of which were written by the children, and 37 illustrations, all drawn by children, as well as a cover by a professional illustrator. Children were able to see the stages of publication and engaged in proofreading as well as drafting, editing and revising. Once published, the book was distributed to all authors, parents, carers and schools at a book launch with a banquet.

Figure 6.6 Cover of *The Wishroom*

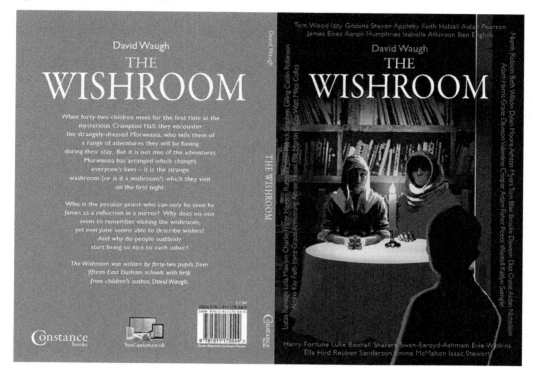

Commentary

Cremin and Myhill's (2012) comments sum up the philosophy behind the project:

> A creatively constructed writing classroom recognises the authority and expertise of the teacher and will include explicit teaching of writing, but this occurs within an environment of democratic participation, where children's voices are heard, where they have ownership of their texts and their decision making, and where they can articulate with confidence their reasons for their writing choices. (Cremin and Myhill 2012: 24)

The production of a novel may be several steps further than most teachers wish to go in writing with and for children, but smaller projects can be developed successfully, especially if the following are borne in mind:

- The teacher needs to model the style of writing and share examples. For instance, there needs to be clarity about use of first or third person and there should be constant consideration of the likely audience for the story.

- Discussion is vital – children need to feel an ownership of the work and that their oral and written contributions are valued.

- Children's contributions can be tailored to their abilities. Children who struggle to write very much might be included as key characters, with the teacher and other children writing with and about them, perhaps drawing upon their oral contributions to write dialogue.

- At every stage, children need to be involved in proofreading, editing and revising, as well as reflecting on their work and discussing ways of improving it. For example, they might consider:

  - vocabulary choices
  - different ways to phrase
  - synonyms to avoid repetition
  - similes to compare things to others
  - metaphors
  - layout – what will appeal to potential readers

- It is also important to pose questions such as:

  - How could this be improved?
  - What do you like/dislike?
  - Which synonyms could be used?
  - Could metaphors or similes be added?
  - Is there too much description and not enough action?
  - Is there too much action and not enough description?

- The structure can be defined by the teacher initially, but might be modified in light of children's ideas.

- The completed work should be presented attractively and shared with its intended readership.

Pause for thought

- How confident do you feel about writing for children?
- If you lack confidence, is this because you are afraid of making mistakes or because you don't feel you have good ideas for writing?
- What would help you to develop your confidence in writing for children?

The illustrations show that it is possible to present children's work attractively and produce something of which they can be proud. The experience of working in this way for over twenty years has shown that where teachers take the trouble to celebrate and publish children's work in this way, children tend to feel inspired to write independently and begin to think of themselves as writers or even authors. There

Figure 6.7 A page from a book, *Instructions on How to Look After Your Dog,* by Kaitlyn in Year 2, who produced this with Rebecca, a trainee teacher

are also clear benefits for the quality of their transcription skills as they see how their words and phrasing can be discussed and, where necessary, corrected before publication. The next section focuses on transcription and looks at ways in which grammatical knowledge can be learnt through writing.

Grammar and writing

It is interesting to note that more children achieved the expected standard in grammar, punctuation and spelling in the 2016 SATs tests (72 per cent) than in reading (66 per cent) (DfE 2016a, b). Yet when the revised curriculum had placed a stronger emphasis upon this area in 2013, there was some concern that what was being demanded was unrealistic both for children and their teachers. Research suggests that there are key strategies which enable successful teaching and learning.

Research focus

Myhill, Lines and Watson (2011) maintained that children were better able to understand the purpose of grammatical knowledge when it was taught in the context of writing rather than in discrete grammar lessons. They argued that

> a writing curriculum which draws attention to the grammar of writing in an embedded and purposeful way at relevant points in the learning is a more positive way forward. In this way, young writers are introduced to what we have called 'a repertoire of infinite possibilities', explicitly showing them how different ways of shaping sentences or texts, and … different choices of words can generate different possibilities for meaning-making. (Myhill et al. 2012: 3)

Reedy and Bearne (2013: 5–6) (see also case study in Chapter 5) found that

> repeated studies show no evidence that formal teaching of grammar out of context has any beneficial effect on either reading or writing. Two significant large-scale studies (Hillocks 1986; Andrews et al. 2006) found no evidence of a relationship. However, more recent projects have involved teaching grammar to support pupils' writing. Working with children aged 6–10 in Scotland, Hunt (2001) has shown that introducing key terms such as "synonym" "verb", "noun", "sentence" and "noun phrase" in the context of shared writing can clarify the options and so help children consider alternative wordings and make appropriate choices.

Pause for thought

- How confident do you feel about teaching each of the following, all of which are part of the curriculum for Year 2: noun, noun phrase, statement, question, exclamation, command, compound, adjective, verb, suffix, adverb, tense (past, present), apostrophe, comma?
- Would you feel confident about using these terms in the context of a writing lesson?

CASE STUDY: Teaching grammar through writing

Beth had attended a CPD course at which the presenter discussed Myhill et al.'s views on teaching grammar through writing. She was concerned that some children in her Year 5 class seemed disengaged during the discrete grammar lessons she had used to teach word classes and other terminology, so she decided to adopt a different approach.

In a shared writing activity, which used a picture of a dark woodland with a crescent moon visible through the trees and two silhouetted figures in the background, Beth modelled writing an opening sentence:

> *The wood was dark and scary and the only light came from a crescent moon.*

She asked the children for their opinion on what she had written, inviting them to suggest ways in which it might be improved. There were suggestions for using different words instead of dark and scary, so Beth made a point of using the word *adjectives* when making a list of possibilities. She also used the word *synonyms* when asking for words with similar meanings.

When she asked children to work in pairs to rewrite the sentence, she found that some changed the order and phrasing so that she was able to talk about clauses and phrases:

> *Gloomy and forbidding, the wood was lit only by a crescent moon.*
> *A crescent moon provided the only illumination in the eerie woods.*

By the time the shared writing had developed into three sentences and children were ready to begin independent and group writing, Beth was able to ask them to explain the following terms, which most children did correctly: *adjective, adverb, noun, synonym, fronted adverbial, clause, phrase*. She also found, as she moved around the room to observe children writing and to discuss their progress, that they were using the terms when talking about their work. She also found that they were much more confident about their meanings and were less likely to confuse adjectives and adverbs and similes and synonyms, etc.

Pause for thought

- Why do you think children seemed more engaged with grammatical terms when they used them as part of writing rather than learning them in discrete grammar lessons?
- Think about a writing lesson you are planning. How can you incorporate meaningful usage of grammatical terminology into the lesson?

Summary

Writing can be a pleasurable activity for children: an opportunity for them to express their ideas and share them with a wider audience. However, they may not achieve this without support, guidance and modelling from experienced writers. Teachers have a vital role to play, not only in providing interesting and varied writing activities but also, crucially, in modelling writing and talking about the strategies they use when developing a piece of writing from the planning stage to publication.

If writing is discussed regularly, there are lots of opportunities to develop children's understanding of grammatical features and the impact their use can have on the quality of their writing. If teachers write for children as well as with them, they will demonstrate that writing is a useful activity and one to be enjoyed.

From reading this chapter you should have a clearer understanding of

- Different approaches to teaching and learning writing and how these can be used to engage children with writing
- Pupil performance in writing and gender differences
- How grammar can be taught through writing
- Modelling writing for children
- Ways in which teachers can write with and for children.

Recommended reading

For ideas for short, imaginative poetry activities, three books by Sandy Brownjohn are full of ideas:

Brownjohn, S. (1980). *Does it Have to Rhyme?* London: Hodder and Stoughton.
Brownjohn, S. (1982). *What Rhymes With Secret?: Teaching Children to Write Poetry.* London: Hodder and Stoughton.
Brownjohn, S. (1994). *To Rhyme or Not to Rhyme.* London: Hodder and Stoughton.

For ideas for writing in every curriculum subject see:

Bushnell, A. and Waugh, D. (2017). *Inviting Writing Across the Curriculum.* London: Sage.

For a range of topics related to developing children's writing once they have mastered the basics see:

Waugh, D., Bushnell, A. and Neaum, S. eds. (2015). *Beyond Early Writing.* Northwich: Critical Publishing.

For stimuli for writing see:

Literacy Shed, http://www.literacyshed.com/the-images-shed.html. This is packed with ideas and resources, including images to use in lessons. (Accessed April 2017).

Chapter 7
Assessing Children in English

Chapter objectives

This chapter will:

- Examine the underlying rationale for different forms of assessment, with a focus on formative assessment, or assessment for learning
- Discuss the implications of assessment without levels
- Cite case studies of how schools are developing new approaches to assessment in English
- Explore peer and self-assessment

The most powerful tool for raising achievement and preparing children to be lifelong learners, in any context, is formative assessment. (Clarke 2014: 3)

Introduction

The complexity of assessment across the four modes of language, speaking and listening, reading and writing, requires both a clear understanding of the rationale for different methods and when to use them, and how to carry these out manageably in the classroom. This chapter will begin by examining different types of assessment, and in the light of the statement from Clarke (2014) above, will focus on the potential of formative assessment. In the context of a very different national system in England, that has moved away from assigning levels to children's attainment, it will discuss how schools have approached this change with a range of case studies. The chapter will also highlight the importance of involving pupils in assessment through either peer or self-assessment. It is only when pupils fully understand what they have succeeded in and why, or why they have not mastered a particular aspect, that they can begin to understand how to improve.

The central importance of teachers having a deep understanding of assessment is emphasized by the review of initial teacher training (DfE 2015b). The report details aspects of assessment that training should include, such as the theories of assessment; important concepts in assessment; stages of development within subjects, so teachers know what to assess; how to use a range of assessment approaches; how to give effective feedback and the next steps for progression. Research has shown that effective assessment is the key to improving learning and Hattie's (2009) meta-analysis of strategies that have the greatest impact on learning highlights that assessment practices and feedback are among the most effective. He cites the effect sizes of different practices (with effect sizes under 0.4 being not worthwhile and anything over 1.0 indicating a child is one year ahead of expectations). Hattie cites the top five strategies as:

1 Assessment literate students: a term used to describe pupils who understand what and how they are learning and can self-assess and improve their learning (effect size 1.44)
2 Providing formative evaluation (effect size 0.90)
3 Lesson study (a professional development tool for teachers to work collaboratively to review learning in lessons) (effect size 0.88)
4 Classroom discussion (to include collaborative learning) (effect size 0.82)
5 Feedback (effect size 0.75)

Hattie (2012: 124) reinforces the importance of feedback (or formative evaluation) saying:

> Feedback is most effective when students do not have proficiency or mastery – and thus it thrives when there is an error or incomplete knowing and understanding…. Errors invite opportunities. They should not be seen as embarrassments, signs of failure, or something to be avoided. They are exciting, because they indicate a tension between what we **now** know and what we **could** know.

For effective feedback to take place, Clarke (2014) cites three principles, derived from Sadler (1989) that the learner should grasp:

1 Possess a concept of the goal being aimed for.
2 Compare the actual level of performance with the goal.
3 Engage in some appropriate action to close the gap.

Feedback also needs to be as immediate as possible and therefore incorporated into the lesson. Clarke (2014: 123) describes using '*mid-lesson learning stops*', that is, reviewing the learning to that point, often using examples of pupils' work. After reviewing examples together, the children should work in pairs to review their own work, using good ideas, words or phrases from the examples, and seeing they can use this to improve their own work. For a short video extract of a teacher doing this, see http://bit.ly/1fnZB5c. You can also see an example of two children cooperatively improving their writing at http://bit.ly/1lZulrY.

Forms of assessment

Black and Wiliam (2009) argued that in spite of widespread use of the term formative assessment and many schools adopting it, there had been no clear rationale developed. Indeed, Clarke (2014) says that she has never seen such confusion over an educational term as 'formative assessment'. Wiliam (2012) noted that the common misinterpretation is that it is about monitoring pupils' learning, whereas it is about pupils becoming owners of their learning. Formative assessment has been likened to assessment *of* learning (AoL), as opposed to summative assessment, which is commonly referred to as assessment *for* learning (AfL). Summative assessment usually occurs at the end of a unit of work, or school phase/year, and may include statutory assessment: it provides information to assist in monitoring pupils' progress and may be used formatively. The next section discusses formative assessment in depth.

Formative assessment

Formative assessment includes a range of assessment procedures by teachers during the learning process to help modify teaching and learning activities to improve pupils' attainment. The Assessment Reform Group (ARG 2000) have set out ten principles that encompass formative assessment (see https://www.aaia.org.uk/content/uploads/2010/06/Assessment-for-Learning- 10-principles.pdf.) and also produced a helpful summary of the role of teachers in the assessment of learning (ARG 2006). They note that fully implementing AfL is challenging for schools because it requires some fundamental changes in practice, such as pupils have ownership over their learning. Use of AfL is not helped by an increasing focus on statutory assessment and the Assessment Reform Group note that national tests have actually '*driven out assessment for learning*' (2006: 9) with a focus on 'teaching to the test', too frequent summative assessment and a lack of a range of evidence to accurately assess pupils' learning.

Black and William's (1998; Wiliam 2000; Black et al. 2003) early work on formative assessment centred on five key strategies:

1 Clarifying and sharing learning intentions and criteria for success criteria with learners.
2 Ensuring effective classroom discussions and other learning tasks that elicit evidence of pupils' understanding.
3 Providing feedback that moves learners forward.
4 Helping pupils to be instructional resources for each other.
5 Activating pupils to be the owners of their own learning.

These aspects have traditionally been associated with the role of the teacher, and a fundamental change in carrying out formative assessment, is the role of the pupils in their own learning and in supporting peers. Black and Wiliam (2009: 8) provide a helpful summary of the respective roles for the teacher, peer and the pupil which are categorized as '*where the learner is going*', '*where the learner is right now*' and '*how to get there*'. What this emphasizes is that it is not only the teacher who needs to make what is being learnt and the progress towards it clear; but also peers need to support each other in developing understanding, and the pupils themselves have a responsibility for their learning.

Black and Wiliam (2009) set out to locate formative assessment within more comprehensive theories of pedagogy, encompassing the teacher's role and the regulation of learning, feedback and student–teacher interaction and the pupil's role in learning. One of the central tenets is the notion of 'moments of contingency', where teachers respond to pupils verbally, or through some form of evidence of learning. These responses can be synchronous or asynchronous and they can help 'close the gap' as Sadler (1989) describes, in order to support learning. Black and Wiliam (2009) also highlight the role of self-regulated learning so that pupils develop good 'habits of mind' (Costa 2008) such as persistence, metacognition, listening with understanding and empathy, questioning and posing problems (see http://www.chsvt.org/wdp/Habits_of_Mind.pdf for a full list). Claxton's work on Building Learning Power (2002) highlights four specific skills that support this: resilience, resourcefulness, reflection and reciprocity.

Clarke (2014) examines the key aspects that are essential to develop formative assessment in the classroom and has expanded on the elements noted above to focus on the culture of the classroom (2014: vii). These key aspects consist of:

- 'Laying the foundations' in which pupils need to be 'active learners, constant reviewers and self-assessors' together with ensuring collaboration between pupils, particularly 'talk partners'.

- Effective starts to lessons in which 'questioning strategies, exploratory activities and examples of pupil work are used to establish prior knowledge, capture interest, co-construct success criteria and discuss excellence'.

- Developing the learning: where 'dialogue is key, establishing and helping children articulate their understanding so far and focusing on constant review and improvement' (2014: vii).

- Effective ends to lessons where various techniques help to encourage pupil reflection, what has been learnt so far and what needs to be developed.

The learning culture that Clarke sets out provides a fundamental shift in practice, in particular in developing collaboration, ownership of learning by pupils and three other fundamental aspects:

1 Developing growth mind-sets, or developing attitudes of mind that encourage pupils to view their ability as capable of growth and not fixed, based on the work of Carol Dweck (2008).

2 Integrating metacognitive strategies. Metacognition describes learning about learning and research has demonstrated its impact (Sutton Trust 2017, cites a potential gain of 8 months).

3 Facilitating mixed-ability learning, rather than children being placed in ability groups, as is common practice in England and which has been shown to be detrimental to progress and children's mind-sets (Sutton Trust 2017; Hattie 2009).

CASE STUDY: Formative assessment in English

In a primary school in the North East of England, the teacher of a Year 6 class begins a lesson as part of a unit of work on suspense writing. The class were reading '*The Nighmare Man*' by Pie Corbett (downloaded from http://www.teachprimary.com/index.php/download/pie-corbett/success). In a previous lesson, the class had discussed the central theme of facing your fears and children talked with partners about any fears they had experienced. After exploring the story in depth over several lessons, acting out scenes and hot-seating activities, the children wrote 'scary' descriptions of night-time before going on to create their own stories on the same theme.

Following independent writing of their stories, the teacher begins the next lesson by showing samples of children's writing produced on the visualizer. Although she had assessed them, they were not annotated. They worked on one example together and then she showed a further example. She explained that the children should work in pairs to read the work and discuss what they would say to the writer. They should identify positive features and offer advice on how to improve it. She gathered the children's responses and used them to draw out some common features they could all use in their writing. They looked particularly at the use of personification, such as 'the angry wind tore into the window pane' as well as the use of short sentences to create suspense. Following this, pupils wrote their revised stories independently. The children's stories were published on the school's website and comments invited which attracted some attention from parents and a local author. As the example below shows, the stories demonstrated many of the features of suspense.

> The thunder echoed around the abandoned house and rain ran down the windows like teardrops. Inside, the house was silent. John crept cautiously into the back door, slipped into the hall and began to search for signs of his sister. Just then a door creaked open. Frozen to the spot, he hid in the shadows.

Pause for thought

1 Why do you think that using examples of the children's writing is a powerful tool for focusing on the features of a particular genre?

2 Consider the role of working in pairs to support writing in this example?

3 What do you consider is the impact of publishing the children's stories on the website?

Research study – factors that inhibit or facilitate formative assessment

A study by Sach (2015) sought to explore the factors that facilitate or inhibit the use of formative assessment practices. A number of themes were derived from interviewing a sample of teachers. These included the notion of prescription where formative assessment was seen as being 'imposed rather than negotiated' (2015: 328). This, Sach claims, helps to explain the findings of Black et al. (2005) where handing down policies ignores the process of implementation and the complexities of different school contexts. Another theme was accountability and all teachers interviewed claimed to be under pressure to meet particular targets for attainment. Such pressure tended to inhibit the use of more formative assessment methods. A further theme was that while there was a shift to more collaborative practices in schools, such as peer/self-assessment, these were not always carried out consistently. In addition, pressures from the leaders of the school often created further demands on teachers so that *formative assessment procedures appear to be lost within systemic conflict'* (Sach 2015: 332).

The study also found facilitating factors in developing formative assessment. These included teacher autonomy and professionalism; and where this was respected, practices were more successful. Providers of training also needed to have credibility in schools and be able to work collaboratively with teachers. Schools also needed to develop shared philosophies about learning within a supportive school ethos, particularly from senior managers and to extend this to networking with other schools.

Pause for thought

1 Consider why ensuring ownership and teacher professionalism is important in developing practices such as formative assessment.

2 What inhibiting factors impacted in this study?

3 Why do you feel networking with other schools could be helpful?

Summative assessment

Summative assessment can be either statutory assessment (Standard Attainment Tests) or non-statutory school-based types of assessment. Both of these are usually carried out at key points, such as at the end of a school year and provide valuable information about a pupil's overall performance to assist in monitoring progress. The Northern Ireland guidance on assessment explores this further and provides some helpful pointers in using summative assessment effectively (CCEA 2013: 6). It recommends that it should:

- *Take account of all the objectives or outcomes of the programme of study/ topic (this is why summative tests of part of the programme of study are not necessarily valid)*
- *Make use of several short assessments rather than the 'big test' at the end of the year*
- *Take account of formative assessments throughout the year, or at the very least in the last term*
- *Be formative in its own right*
- *Provide feedback on what learners did or did not do well*
- *Provide teachers with insights into what pupils have and have not learnt in order to adjust and refine their teaching*

The Northern Ireland guidance provides support on methods of using summative assessment to improve learning. For further information, see http://www. nicurriculum.org.uk/docs/key_stages_1_and_2/areas_of_learning/Guidance_on_ Assessment_Primary.pdf, particularly page 7.

Assessment without levels

After the publication of the National Curriculum (DfE 2013), the government set up a commission to review assessment practices. The report stated that the use of levels had resulted in a '*profoundly negative impact on teaching*' (c, 2015b: 5) and stated that:

> Too often levels became viewed as thresholds and teaching became focused on getting pupils across the next threshold instead of ensuring they were secure in the knowledge and understanding defined in the programmes of study. Depth and breadth of understanding were sometimes sacrificed in favour of pace. (DfE 2015c: 5)

In the introduction to the report, John McIntosh, the Chair of the Commission, comments:

> The changes to the National Curriculum and its assessment go well beyond mere changes of content. They invoke very different day-to-day approaches to assessment and signal fundamental shifts in ideas about learning and assessment. (DfE 2015c: 3)

The report made the following recommendations:

- The setting up of a standing committee on assessment, supported by a panel of experts
- That assessment is a core part of initial teacher training
- The establishment of a national item bank of assessment questions to help both formative assessment and for summative assessment by enabling teachers to create bespoke tests for assessment at the end of a topic or teaching period and the establishment of an online forum for teachers to share assessment ideas

- The development of a training module for senior leaders to ensure a shared understanding of the principles of assessment
- The setting up of a review group for school data management
- Establishing an expert group for assessment of pupils who are working below the levels of the National Curriculum tests, including a review of the former P-Scales.

Interim assessment frameworks

Since the publication of the report on assessment without levels, the DfE has developed interim teacher assessment frameworks for 2016 and 2017 to support teachers in making robust and accurate judgements for pupils at the end of key stages 1 and 2. The Department for Education points out that this is a temporary arrangement and it is evaluating options for future years. The key points to note in these interim frameworks for reading and writing are set out below.

(1) Reading

At KS1 there are three performance descriptors – 'working towards the national standard', 'working at the national standard' and 'working at a greater depth within the national standard'. At KS2, there is just one: 'working at the national standard'. Achievement above this level would be reflected in a child's scaled score from the Year 6 reading test.

At KS1, word reading requires that children read accurately and fluently, 'sounding out unfamiliar words accurately and without undue hesitation'. It is this fluency by the end of Year 2 that may form a major focus for schools.

At KS2, where the performance descriptors take ability to read words as a given, the focus in on comprehension, with children being expected to read 'whole novels'.

The performance descriptors are not designed to be used in the same way as the previous Assessing Pupil Progress (APP) statements, which often led to a list printed out and then highlighted when a child achieves each statement three times. Instead, they show some of the key elements of reading children need to be able to demonstrate they can do by the end of the key stage. It shows children need to be assessed in a much more holistic way, assessing two or more descriptors together, rather than each one forming the basis of a discrete learning objective. All of these aspects of reading are interlinked.

(2) Writing

At both KS1 and KS2 there are three performance descriptors – 'working towards the national standard', 'working at the national standard' and 'working at greater depth within the national standard'. The descriptors are for describing where a child is working at the end of the key stage. They are not designed to be applied to a single piece of writing and aims to give feedback to help children to improve their writing, rather than just giving their work a label.

The most significant change from the previous system of levels is that these performance descriptors are **not** to be used in a 'best fit' way. To demonstrate that pupils have met the standard, teachers will need to have evidence that a pupil demonstrates consistent attainment of **all** the statements within the standard.

The majority of the objectives mention skills and knowledge linked to spelling, punctuation, grammar or handwriting. For 'working at the national standard' at KS1 these elements make up all twelve criteria, which should be demonstrated through writing a narrative. At KS2, it is nine out of ten across a range of purposes and audiences. The descriptors need to be applied to a range of different pieces of writing, rather than a single piece.

These performance descriptors are not designed to replace the National Curriculum, or to be treated as the basis for teaching writing. They are for a snapshot assessment, and schools should still teach the breadth of the curriculum.

For detailed information, see https://www.gov.uk/government/publications/2017-interim-frameworks-for-teacher-assessment-at-the-end-of-key-stage-1 and https://www.gov.uk/government/publications/2017-interim-frameworks-for-teacher-assessment-at-the-end-of-key-stage-2

Schools' approaches

Schools have adopted a number of different approaches to this fundamental change in not using National Curriculum levels. The National College for Teaching and Leadership (NCTL) undertook a research project working with Teaching School alliances to examine different approaches. The report of the project found that

> the consensus from participating schools about the importance of formative classroom assessment has been further supported in these research projects. (NCTL 2014: 5)

The report notes that the concept of formative assessment or assessment for learning has been understood by these schools as '*assessment for teaching*' (2014: 5). It also notes that a number of assessment tools have been developed including taxonomy grids, progressive mastery statements and marking grids. The use of technology to track pupils' progress was also a feature. Some of the approaches noted in this research are summarized below.

1 Visible learning approaches: based on the work of Hattie (2012). This is a focus on ensuring that teachers make it clear, what they are teaching and why and what pupils should be learning. This clarity, or visibility, helps improve pupil achievement. This approach has led to schools making

learning and teaching more explicit, including the use of self- and peer-assessment strategies. Another linked approach is SOLO (the Structure of the Observed Learning Outcomes), which is widely used in New Zealand. This approach maps the complexity of a pupil's work by linking it to one of five phases: little or no understanding (Prestructural), through a simple and then more developed grasp of the topic (Unistructural and Multistructural), to the ability to link the ideas and elements of a task together (Relational) and finally (Extended Abstract) to understand the topic for themselves, possibly going beyond the initial scope of the task. For more information, see http://pamhook.com/solo-taxonomy/.

2 Revised Bloom's taxonomy

Some schools have developed a version of Bloom's knowledge and cognitive processes to classify objectives, activities and assessments which they then used to improve curriculum planning and their teaching. The revised taxonomy (Krathwohl 2002) is a two-dimensional framework: knowledge and cognitive processes, which when combined form a very useful reference table. Using the table to classify objectives, activities and assessments provides a clear, concise visual representation of a particular course or unit.

3 Mastery Statements

Schools in the study were keen to involve pupils in formative assessment using mastery statements. These often take the form of 'I can' grids which are directly related to the National Curriculum, examples of these can be found in NCTL (2014) '*Beyond levels – alternative approaches by teaching schools*'. Schools also developed skills ladders, milestones or smaller steps such as '*inch pebbles*'. Learning ladders is an online tool which helps schools to create their own curriculum and to define pupil progress using 'ladders' to mark stages in a child's development (see http://www.learningladders.info).

4 Curriculum Progression Objectives

Progression objectives for mathematics and English have been developed by some alliances. This drew on examples produced by the National Association of Headteachers (NAHT) to develop detailed mini-statements of achievement and provided opportunities for children to self-assess alongside the teachers' judgement.

Schools have found a number of ways to respond to the changes in assessment following the publication of the National Curriculum in 2014. One of the key advantages has been a review of assessment practices and help in establishing better use of formative assessment.

It is also useful to be aware of other tools that can support assessment such as the Centre for Language and Primary Education (CLPE) writing and reading scales available free from https://www.clpe.org.uk/library-and-resources/reading-and-writing-scales. The CLPE (n.d.) states that The CLPE Reading and Writing Scales *'describe the journey that children make in order to become literate'*. They are designed to show progression and not to be summative and to help support teachers' subject knowledge of literacy. These were originally published over 30 years ago as part of the CLPE Primary Language Record and they have been completely updated by the CLPE together with the with English and Media Centre (EMC), National Association for Advisors in English (NAAE) and the National Association for the Teaching of English (NATE) and United Kingdom Literacy Association (UKLA) to reflect recent research.

Peer and self-assessment

Peer and self-assessment are effective ways of supporting children to understand their progress in learning and to identify the next steps. The aim is to involve children in constructive criticism of their work and to build time into lessons to do this.

However, putting this into practice effectively in the classroom is not straightforward. Boon's action research study (2016) found that children were frustrated with peer assessment because they felt their peers did not always pay attention to their comments and it relied on their understanding of how to write helpful feedback. Wiliam (2011b: 12) argues that 'feedback is useless unless it is acted upon'.

Studies show that children need training in giving good quality feedback (Topping 2009, 2010) and need to have opportunities to discuss it plus have time to respond and act on this feedback. Boon (2016) sought to put these key points into practice with a study of his own Year 6 class. His findings showed that the children's uptake of peer feedback increased because of the following factors:

- *It was more useful for assessees*
- *They had time to use it to improve the quality of work*
- *They were allowed to discuss feedback with one another to clarify any misunderstandings about its content*
- *Pupils had become more thoughtful about how the feedback could be used through*
- *The reflection sheet provided*

(Boon 2016: 216)

Peer assessment is usually introduced to young children before self-assessment, as this helps them to develop the ability to give constructive criticism to their classmates, before applying it to their own work. In self-assessment, children are able to take the lessons they have learnt from peer assessment and apply them to their own work to effectively establish an insight into their own performance. Schools have found that in implementing peer and self-assessment, it is helpful to go through clear steps as follows:

1 Preparation

This involves ensuring that children have the necessary skills of self-awareness, listening skills, questioning skills and their ability to empathize and manage feelings, only then can they maximize the benefits of peer and self-assessment.

2 Modelling

It is important for excellent modelling of the assessment process together with the appropriate language before children can do this themselves. Clarke (2008) recommends that the process should move from shared modelling of the process to peer assessment, followed by self-assessment.

3 Practice

Daily practice of peer and self-assessment works best when specific opportunities are planned in lessons. Clarke (2008) recommends asking children to share/peer evaluate a text before writing so that the pupils can see what success looks like and from this, set their own criteria for success. Clarke also recommends beginning the process with simple strategies such as traffic lights (red, amber and green denoting different levels of success) and swapping work and marking it.

Black and Wiliam (1998) argue that self-assessment by pupils is an essential component of formative assessment. Bourke (2016: 99) argues it is important for self-assessment to be seen:

> more broadly as a pedagogical tool, an assessment and learning approach, and a metacognitive strategy where learning rather than measurement is the focus, the notion of reflective intelligence is foregrounded.

One of the issues with peer and self-assessment is the focus on pre-determined objectives. As Swaffield (2008) argues it becomes a 'tyranny of objectives'. Eisner (2002) encourages a more open interpretation of understanding what has been learned and where to go next and uses the analogy of a design specification given to an architect for a house where certain features are specified but the final form is not. Swaffield states (2008: 6):

> Assessment for learning when the learner is centre stage is equally, if not more, suited to fuzzy outcomes, horizons of possibilities, problem-solving and evaluative objectives, as it is to tightly specified curriculum objectives matched to prescribed standards. It is the (mis)interpretation of AfL as a teacher driven mechanism for advancing students up a prescribed ladder of subject attainment that is the problem, not AfL itself. At the heart of this problem is the understanding of teachers' and learners' roles in AfL.

This creates some fundamental changes in culture in the classroom so that the roles of the teacher and learner alter from the traditional view of the teacher as the fount of all knowledge to the pupils having ownership of their learning.

Peer critique is another form of peer-assessment and as discussed in Chapter 2, it can be a powerful tool when implemented carefully. This concept stems from the work of Ron Berger (2003); the core of which is an insistence that if a piece of work isn't perfect it isn't finished (see pages 23–34). The case study: embedding a mastery teaching approach (page 23) demonstrates that when feedback is carefully considered and as in this case includes, adult, peer and teacher feedback, it helped to support children to make small changes to each draft of a piece of work and improve it each time.

CASE STUDY: Peer assessment of writing

At a primary school in York, children work in groups to review their writing. Using a list of objectives that children have discussed, they use these to judge whether their peers' writing demonstrates these features. Having read their own writing and that of a peer, children ask each other questions about the work based on the objectives. They are aiming to meet all the objectives to ensure that they are demonstrating some evidence that they are working above expectations. Following this, the children work in pairs to write targets to help improve their writing. They understand that they need to make the targets appropriate and manageable. This helps everyone to see how they are improving and they understand the next steps in improving their writing. The impact has been to not only improve the standards of writing, but also to improve self-esteem and engagement with writing. The comments made by the teacher when marking are also easier to understand.

Pause for thought

1 Why is it necessary for the children to have discussed the objectives?

2 In what ways does peer work here support understanding?

3 Why is it important for the children to devise targets for improvement?

A series of documents produced in 2015 by the National Association of Advisers in English (NAAE), the National Association for the Teaching of English (NATE) and the United Kingdom Literacy Association (UKLA) aimed to produce a 'better plan' for the assessment and teaching of English. It offers a complete alternative curriculum for the Early Years Foundation Stage and for key stages 1 to 4. The plan also critiques the Department for Education's arrangements for assessment and examinations across the 3 to 19 age range and proposes alternatives which would provide

> reliable information as to learners' progress, while representing a more fruitful relationship between curriculum and assessment than do many of the current and planned statutory requirements. (2015: 4)

At the time of writing, it is too early to judge the reaction to this approach to the curriculum and assessment; however, in reviewing assessment practices in schools, it may act as a valuable contribution to the discussion.

Summary

Developing effective assessment practices, particularly formative assessment, revolves around the learning culture of the classroom. There are key aspects to be considered such as the teacher's role; the use of dialogue to support learning; the pupils' role as active learners; the regulation of learning; pupil–teacher interaction and the use of feedback. These can help to achieve what Sadler (1989) calls 'closing the gap' in learning. Swaffield (2008: 2) describes a more positive picture of assessment:

> The word 'assessment' has its roots in the Latin verb assidere meaning 'to sit beside', a notion somewhat removed from conceptions of assessment that give prominence to examination and testing. The picture of someone sitting besides a learner, perhaps in dialogue over a piece of work, represents much more accurately assessment as a support for learning rather than assessment as a test of performance.

As this chapter has shown, practices of assessment are under review in schools and many new approaches are being developed. It is hoped that the move to assessment without levels will provide opportunities for more effective methods that move away from any tendency to focus too much on summative assessment and the dangers of teaching to the test.

In this chapter you will have developed your knowledge and understanding of:

- The rationale for different forms of assessment, with a focus on the value of formative assessment, or assessment for learning
- The implications of assessment without levels
- Examples of how schools are developing new approaches to assessment in English
- The use of peer and self-assessment

Recommended reading

For a detailed review of classroom practices that support formative assessment see:

Clarke, S. (2014). *Outstanding Formative Assessment: Culture and Practice*. London: Hodder Education.

For examples of schools approaches to assessment without levels see:

National College for Teaching and leadership (NCTL) (2014). *Beyond Levels: Alternative Assessment Approaches Developed by Teaching Schools. Research Report*. https://www.gov.uk/government/uploads/system/uploads/attachment_data/file/349266/beyond-levels-alternative-assessment-approaches-developed- by-teaching-schools.pdf

For a meta-analysis of the impact of different approaches in schools see:

Hattie, J. (2009). *Visible Learning: A Synthesis of Over 800 meta-Analyses Relating to Achievement*. London: Routledge.

Chapter 8
Practical Issues: Challenges for Trainee and Beginner Teachers

Learning objectives for this chapter

By reading this chapter you will develop your understanding of the following:

- Identifiable qualities of effective teachers, with a particular focus on primary English
- Some of the challenges trainees and beginner teachers might face in primary English
- Some practical solutions to challenges

Introduction

In this chapter, we will look at challenges for trainee and beginner teachers by focusing initially on what research tells us about the qualities which produce good teaching. We will look at the teaching of primary English in the context of these qualities and will explore strategies which can enable us to become effective teachers. Case study examples will show how trainees and new teachers have tackled issues related to the quality of their teaching, and there will be examples of research undertaken to discover more about what constitutes good teaching.

Research focus

Coe et al. (2014) examined research on teaching quality and identified six common components whose extensive research indicated were key factors in determining teaching quality. They listed these approaches, skills and knowledge in order of how strong the evidence is in showing that focusing on them can improve student outcomes. They assert that high-quality teaching will include a combination of these attributes and that the best teachers are those who demonstrate all of these features.

1 **(Pedagogical) Content knowledge (strong evidence of impact on student outcomes)**

   The most effective teachers have deep knowledge of the subjects they teach, and when teachers' knowledge falls below a certain level it is a significant impediment to students' learning. As well as a strong understanding of the material being taught, teachers must also understand the ways students think about the content, be able to evaluate the thinking behind students' own methods and identify students' common misconceptions.

2 **Quality of instruction (strong evidence of impact on student outcomes)**

   It includes elements such as effective questioning and use of assessment by teachers. Specific practices, like reviewing previous learning, providing model responses for students, giving adequate time for practice to embed skills securely and progressively introducing new learning (scaffolding) are also elements of high-quality instruction.

3 **Classroom climate (moderate evidence of impact on student outcomes)**

   It covers quality of interactions between teachers and students, and teacher expectations: the need to create a classroom that is constantly demanding more, but still recognizing students' self-worth. It also involves attributing student success to effort rather than ability and valuing resilience to failure (grit).

4 **Classroom management (moderate evidence of impact on student outcomes)**

   A teacher's abilities to make efficient use of lesson time, to coordinate classroom resources and space, and to manage students' behaviour with clear rules that are consistently enforced, are all relevant to maximizing the learning that can take place. These environmental factors are necessary for good learning rather than its direct components.

5 **Teacher beliefs (some evidence of impact on student outcomes)**

   Why teachers adopt particular practices, the purposes they aim to achieve, their theories about what learning is and how it happens and their conceptual models of the nature and role of teaching in the learning process all seem to be important.

6 **Professional behaviours (some evidence of impact on student outcomes)**

   Behaviours exhibited by teachers such as reflecting on and developing professional practice, participation in professional development, supporting colleagues and liaising and communicating with parents.

Coe et al. (2014: 2–3)

Pause for thought

Consider the qualities identified by Coe et al.:

- Which do you feel are already your strengths?
- Which do you need to work on?
- Do you have a sense of what you need to do if you are to develop your teaching in these areas?

Content or subject knowledge

In Chapter 4, we looked at Cremin et al.'s work on teachers' knowledge of children's literature and poetry. It was clear that where teachers lacked knowledge of literature, children's progress could be hampered. The same is true of many other aspects of primary English teaching. In this section we will focus on an element which has proved particularly challenging for many teachers following various changes to the curriculum: grammar. You will find more detailed discussion about grammar in Chapter 5 and in Chapter 6 you can read about teaching grammar through writing. For many teachers, however, it is not grammar that they find difficult to understand; it is the terminology associated with it.

Why do we need to know terminology?

If you do not feel very confident about using grammatical terms, there are plenty of places where you can find help, including books, websites and apps (see the end of chapter). You may feel some resentment that you now have to teach terminology which you were not taught at school and might even feel that it is unnecessary, given that you managed to become a literate and successful person without it.

If we understand some basic terminology associated with our language, we have a shortcut for description, just as we do in other subjects such as maths. We don't have to describe the concept each time we refer to an aspect of grammar. So, for example, when teachers used to talk about using 'describing words' rather than using the term adjectives, they were avoiding a term which would have been easy to remember, and were also being imprecise, given that adverbs are also describing words: adjectives describe or qualify nouns, while adverbs describe or modify verbs. Thus in the sentence below, the adjective heavy describes the bag, while the adverb slowly tells us how Joe walked by modifying the verb.

Joe walked slowly because he was carrying a heavy bag.

What do we need to know?

We all know lots about English grammar, even if we cannot always use terminology to describe we know what. For example, you probably noticed that the last three words of the previous sentence were in the wrong order. You may have paused and read them again, perhaps thinking there had been a misprint. Or you may have subconsciously changed the order of the words because you read quickly and expect what you read to make sense.

The English National Curriculum for English states the following:

> Throughout the programmes of study, teachers should teach pupils the vocabulary they need to discuss their reading, writing and spoken language. It is important that pupils learn the correct grammatical terms in English and that these terms are integrated within teaching. (DfE 2013: 15)

There are numerous terms which you will need to understand and be able to use when you are teaching, but we provide below definitions of four key terms which are often used when we talk about language.

Grammar

Grammar refers to a set of rules about how we use language. It covers such things as how to form words, by adding prefixes or suffixes to refine the meaning or to change the job a word is doing in a sentence, and how to arrange words to convey clear meaning.

Syntax

Syntax means the rules that define the ordering and arrangement of words within a phrase or sentence to ensure that the reader or listener understands clearly what the user meant. Syntax is a subset of grammar, and the two words are often used interchangeably.

Punctuation

Punctuation is the study of the different ways in which a passage of language can be broken up into shorter units, for example by using commas or full-stops, and the ways in which effects of speech such as surprise or doubt can be indicated in written language.

Usage

Usage refers to the customary or common way that language is used, rather than to strict definitions which are sometimes out of date. We might say that 'usage is divided' over the pronunciation of the word *economics*, or that terms like *fake news* and *Brexit have* become 'common usage'.

Quality of instruction

By the time you read this you will doubtless have observed teachers whose practice seems almost effortless. Their classes are attentive and know what is expected of them and the teacher makes the lesson content seem interesting and worth studying. These teachers make good use of questioning and seem able to tease out who understands concepts and who needs support. You may also have observed teachers who were less successful and whose classes were less engaged. Medwell et al. (1998) looked closely at effective teachers of literacy and identified some key features which they exhibited.

Research focus: Effective teachers of literacy

Medwell et al. (1998) found that effective teachers had the following attributes:

Pace and timing

All the teachers taught letter sounds but the effective teachers tended to teach within the context of using a text. They also tended to use short, regular teaching sessions, often involving them in modelling to the children how sounds worked. They placed less emphasis on paper exercises.

The lessons of the effective teachers were all conducted at a brisk pace. They regularly re-focused children's attention on the task at hand and used clear time frames to keep children on task. Many concluded their lessons by reviewing, with the whole class, what the children had done during the lesson.

Differentiation

Some effective teachers differentiated the work they asked pupils to do by allotting different tasks on the basis of ability. These teachers also varied the support given to particular groups of children when they were engaged on tasks the whole class would do at some point. By this means they were able to keep their classes working more closely together through a programme of work.

Assessment

The effective teachers had very clear assessment procedures, usually involving a great deal of focused observation and systematic record-keeping. This contributed markedly to their abilities to select appropriate literacy content for their children's needs.

Pause for thought

- What good examples of pace and timing, differentiation, and assessment have you observed?
- How do effective teachers maintain children's attention?
- Have you observed differentiation in planning, where children of different abilities are given different tasks, as well as differentiation by outcome, where everyone performs the same task but the outcomes vary according to ability?
- How do effective teachers use assessment to inform their planning?

Look again at Chapter 2 and consider how adopting a mastery approach to teaching and learning might have an impact on differentiation and assessment.

Commentary

Extensive research over many years has enabled educators to identify certain qualities which successful teachers tend to exhibit. It is worth reflecting upon your own teaching to decide to what extent you incorporate such qualities into your work. It is also important to observe experienced teachers and to consider how they achieve success for their pupils.

Rosenshine (2010) examined more than 40 years of research on effective instruction and distilled this into ten key principles:

1 Begin a lesson with a short review of previous learning
2 Present new material in small steps, with student practice after each step
3 Ask a large number of questions and check the responses of all students
4 Provide models for problem solving and worked examples
5 Guide student practice
6 Check for student understanding
7 Obtain a high success rate

8 Provide scaffolds for difficult tasks

9 Require and monitor independent practice

10 Engage students in weekly and monthly review

(see Coe et al. 2014: 14–15)

Pause for thought

- Look at each of the principles above and reflect on the extent to which your own practice matches them.
- Consider what you need to do to develop those aspects where you do not consider your practice is strong.

Classroom climate

The climate of a classroom can refer to the way in which teachers and pupils interact and can also include the environment which the teacher creates in order to develop a productive working setting. This can demand a lot from both teachers and pupils and developing an ethos whereby good work is celebrated and pupils' self-esteem is raised. The physical environment of a classroom can be a good indicator of the attitudes and beliefs of the teacher and can show children the value which is placed upon their learning. The case study below shows the importance of reviewing classroom environments and sharing good practice.

Figure 8.1 Reception children took part in a topic involving a 'magic carpet ride' which took them to Brazil to see Carnival

CASE STUDY: Creating a 'literate' classroom

Kulwinder was newly appointed as literacy coordinator at a 250-pupil primary school in an inner city area. At interview she had been asked to identify some areas which her visit to the school had led her to wish to improve. She had commented on the fact that some classrooms did not display examples of children's writing but did have several displays of vocabulary and definitions of grammatical terms, while others had several displays of children's work, but few displays which might act as reference points for children.

Upon taking up her post, Kulwinder decided that if she was to get a balance of celebrating and supporting children's work it would be important for teachers to look critically at the classrooms and then discuss good practice and how it might be developed by all. When it was her turn to lead a curriculum meeting after school, Kulwinder prepared some simple evaluation sheets and asked teachers to go to each classroom in the school independently and to make brief notes on at least one example of good practice and one thing which might be done to create a better literacy environment.

After spending around 45 minutes touring the school, teachers reconvened and were asked to work in small groups, each of which included someone from each key stage and to discuss what they had seen. Kulwinder was anxious to avoid making anyone feel criticized and so when the groups were asked to report back to the whole staff to share their findings, they were asked to focus only on good practice at this stage. The discussions were lively and positive and at the end Kulwinder asked each teacher to identify at least one thing they would do in the short term and one in the medium term to make their classroom a better environment for English.

Figure 8.2 A writing wall in Year 2

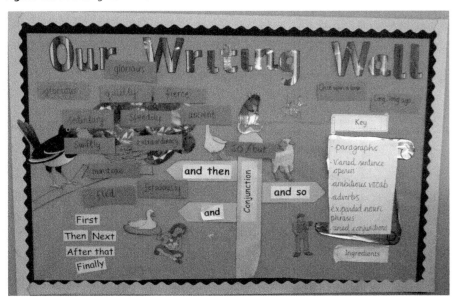

Figure 8.3 A working wall for English in Year 5

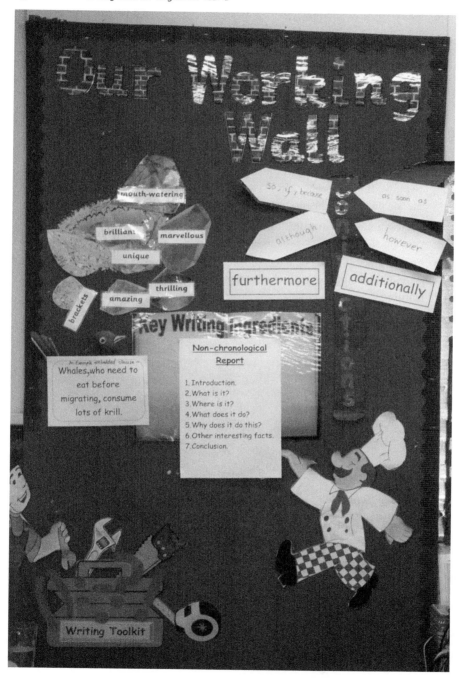

As a result of the review, the school developed a display policy which included some key values:

- All classrooms should have displays which can be used to support learning and act as reference points during independent work.
- Displays of work should appear inside classrooms, but should mainly be placed in corridors and other areas of the school so that they can be viewed by all pupils, staff and visitors.

Suggestions

- When visiting other classrooms and schools, make a note of good ideas for displays. If appropriate, ask if you can photograph examples so that you can use the pictures as inspirations for your own displays.
- Photograph your own displays and keep a portfolio of good examples which you can show at interviews.
- Ensure you achieve a balance between displaying children's work and providing useful displays which can support your teaching and children's learning.

Figure 8.4 A working wall for English in Year 6

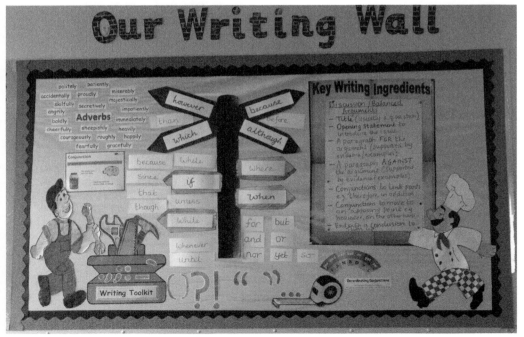

Figure 8.5 One teacher collected spelling errors and displayed these in her Year 6 classroom and challenged children to spot the mistakes and write the notices correctly

Figure 8.5 Continued

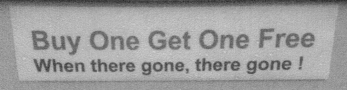

Classroom management for English

This section will examine some of the challenges teachers may face in managing literacy lessons. Many of the challenges and possible solutions are generic and could apply to any subject, but some are specific to literacy. The case study below illustrates some of these.

CASE STUDY: Class management in a writing lesson

Ranjit had made a promising start to a placement with a Year 5 class in a large suburban school. He had established good relationships with the children and the class teacher had complimented him on the quality of his planning and his general attitude. However, the first two writing lessons he took had not gone so well and he had felt pressured by children's constant requests for help and by the general noise levels in the classroom, which he felt accounted for the limited amounts of writing produced by many children.

Ranjit discussed his concerns with the classteacher, who suggested he observe the teacher in the parallel class who was noted for being able to get her children to produce high-quality writing. Ranjit arranged this and asked if he could simply observe rather than getting involved in the lesson, as he wanted to see how a teacher managed a whole class with minimal support (the class had a TA for one child who was on the autism spectrum).

Ranjit enjoyed watching a successful lesson in which the class continued writing stories they had begun in the previous lesson, and noted the following:

- The objectives and success criteria for the lesson were made clear at the beginning of the lesson, which began with the teacher talking positively about examples of the children's writing from the previous lesson. She drew attention to the qualities of the work, but also spent time talking about common misconceptions, such as misuse of possessive apostrophes, and things she would like to see in the current lesson, including more use of subordinate clauses.

- Children were given opportunities to discuss about their work, but these were interspersed with periods of quiet writing.

- Children did not leave their tables to ask for help. If they could not spell a word they had a try at it or wrote as much as they could in pencil and then discussed it with the teacher when she came to their table.

- The teacher patrolled the classroom to provide individual support and to talk to groups, while occasionally stopping the whole class to share good work and good use of subordinate clauses by reading extracts from children's work aloud.

- Instead of repeatedly telling children they were too noisy, as Ranjit had done in his last writing lesson, the teacher adopted a more positive approach by praising good working habits and stopping the class to discuss their work when noise levels began to rise. Ranjit could see that the atmosphere in the classroom and the children's attitude to their writing was much more positive than in his lessons. The quality of the work was also, on the whole, higher than his class had achieved.

The teacher was delighted with the comments Ranjit made after the lesson and offered to observe his next writing lesson if she could arrange this with his classteacher.

Pause for thought

- Why do you think the teacher's writing lesson was successful?
- How might you modify your own writing lessons in light of what you have read?

Now look at the research evidence below on teaching Year 5 and consider ways in which the teacher's practice demonstrated some of the qualities described.

Research focus: Teaching Year 5

Siraj-Blatchford et al. (2011: 1) conducted observations in 82 Year 5 classrooms and found that Year 5 teachers in excellent schools (defined as those which are academically effective with good quality pedagogy) exhibited the following:

Organizational skills: Teachers share clear learning objectives with their pupils, ensure all pupils understand the objectives and associated concepts, have extremely well-organized resources and well-established classroom routines.

Established a positive classroom climate: Relationships between children and between adults and children are characterized by a sense of liking and mutual respect, classrooms are happy places, children are less disruptive and behaviour management is handled sensitively.

Personalized their teaching: Teachers are sensitive to the needs and interests of their pupils, provide a variety of resources to suit the individuals in their classes are more likely to make explicit the links between learning in the classroom and the world outside the classroom and provide homework directly linked to what children are learning in their lessons.

Used dialogic teaching and learning: Children work collaboratively, take part in instructional conversations in literacy, have opportunities to receive evaluative feedback and spend more time learning and performing analysis. In Maths, these teachers use analysis and maths discourse, share maths 'authority' with the children and their pupils have greater depth of knowledge and understanding.

Made more frequent and better use of the plenary: Teachers in the best schools are about twice as likely as teachers in poor schools to use a plenary and they use it to provide feedback and to allow further discussion, exploration and extension.

Although there are similarities here to Coe et al., Siraj-Blatchford et al. (2011) include some aspects of teaching not implied but not necessarily highlighted by Coe et al., including using dialogic teaching and making good use of the plenary. It is worth considering how you can make use of discussion to help children evaluate their learning. Plenary sessions are often rushed and limited to a quick review or sharing what some children have done. It is important to set aside sufficient time for meaningful dialogue to take place. This could involve some discussion between groups of children, as well as interaction with the teacher. It should also be an opportunity for children to talk about how well they met the learning outcomes and what they need to do next if they are to improve their performance further.

Pause for thought

- Think about lessons you have taught and observed in which the plenary was used effectively. What were the key factors which led to success?

Beliefs about teaching primary English

Your beliefs about teaching and learning will continue to evolve as you gain more experience, attend professional development courses and observe and discuss other people's teaching.

Research focus: Literacy teachers' beliefs

Wray et al. (2003) investigated the links between teachers' beliefs about literacy teaching and their choice of teaching approaches. They concluded:

The effective teachers of literacy tended to place a high value upon communication and composition in their views about the teaching of reading and writing: that is, they believed that the creation of meaning in literacy was fundamental. They were more coherent in their belief systems about the teaching of literacy and tended to favour teaching activities which explicitly emphasised the deriving and the creating of meaning. In much of their teaching they were at pains to stress to pupils the purposes and functions of reading and writing tasks. (p. 104)

Pause for thought

Effective teachers, then, not only have strong beliefs about what is important in teaching and learning literacy, but also convey these beliefs to their pupils. This could be done partly through creating a productive classroom climate, as shown above, but also involves conveying to children the value of what they are being asked to do and emphasizing the importance of meaning.

- What examples have you seen of teachers with strong beliefs about teaching literacy?
- How effectively did these teachers work with their pupils?
- If you were asked at interview to describe your philosophy of teaching primary English, what would you say?

Look again at Chapter 3 on creativity and consider, in particular, Jeffrey's (2006) study of creative features of classrooms.

- To what extent do your beliefs about teaching primary English include the four key aspects that characterize creative teaching and learning: relevance, control, ownership and innovation?

Professional behaviours

To exemplify good practice in this category, the focus will be on working with parents. The final Teachers' Standard (DfE 2012), *8. Fulfil wider professional responsibilities*, includes: *Communicate effectively with parents with regard to pupils' achievements and well-being*. As Doherty and Waugh (2017: 211) maintained: 'Primary-aged children spend at most about 15 per cent of their time in school, which means the majority of time is spent at home with their parents. Parents are the child's first educators.' Desforges and Abouchaar (2003) maintained that 'parental involvement has a significant effect on children's achievement and adjustment even after all other factors (such as social class, maternal education and poverty) have been taken out of the equation between children's aptitudes and their achievement' (p. 4).

Working with parents is, then, an important element of the teacher's role and it is essential to adopt an inclusive approach. In 2001 Close reported in an executive summary of research on parental involvement that 'some parents are at risk of "exclusion" from interventions because of their own reading difficulties or because of different language and cultural backgrounds' (p. 5).

This means that we need to communicate clearly and regularly so that we can work with parents for the benefit of their children. Teachers possess expertise in literacy and have been trained in teaching aspects such as reading, spelling and grammar. Parents and carers' knowledge is likely to be less sophisticated, but they know their children well and are usually willing to support teachers by working with their children outside school hours.

CASE STUDY: Creating a spelling leaflet for parents

Many schools produce concise brochures which explain simple strategies for helping children. For example, one school which regularly sent children home with lists of spellings to learn responded to some parents' comments that they would like some strategies by producing a leaflet of one sheet of A4 paper folded and printed on both sides. Simple strategies for learning spellings and approaches to working with children were provided, including:

Look-say-cover-write-check

This is a simple strategy for learning to spell a word. Look at the word carefully and at the sequence of letters; say the word aloud; cover it up; try to write it correctly; check to see if you were right. If you were, move on to another word; if you weren't, go through the process again.

Identify and learn the 'tricky' bits

English words often have 'tricky' bits and we can identify them when making our first attempts at writing the words. For example, the word *separate* is often misspelled as 'seperate' so the tricky bit is remembering to use an a not an e after the p. Most parts of most words are very regular so we can focus our attention on the bits we might misspell rather than spending lots of time on bits we would spell correctly anyway.

The leaflet included other strategies and some general guidance on helping with spelling, including working in short sessions and not trying to make children learn when they were tired.

Comments

If you want to produce similar guidance for parents and carers, it can be helpful to involve some and get them to give feedback on what you produce. Remember that you use a lot of terminology which is part of your everyday working life and that parents may not necessarily understand terms or acronyms connected with teaching, just as you might not understand terminology they use in their working lives.

> ## Pause for thought
>
> Make brief notes on the guidance you could provide to help parents and carers to support children's reading. Tailor this to a particular year group or key stage.
>
> - Which messages are essential?
> - Which terminology will require explanation?
> - How would you present the guidance – online on the school's website, on paper, or in some other way?

Harris and Goodall's (2007: 1) summary of research included:

> Parental engagement is a powerful lever for raising student achievement in schools. Where parents and teachers work together to improve learning, the gains in achievement are significant.

If this is to be achieved, teachers need to be able to convey clearly children's levels of progress and discuss these in an informed manner with parents and carers. This means keeping detailed records with examples of children's work, and it involves knowing what children like reading and their attitudes to reading and writing, as well as their confidence with spelling, grammar and punctuation and their oral contributions. At a parents' meeting it won't be sufficient to say that a child is 'doing quite well with reading': you will need to be specific about what she can do and what she could do with support, as well as talking about the kind of texts she likes and perhaps recommending some she might try at home. If there are specific aspects of literacy, such as some grapheme–phoneme correspondences, which require attention, parents can be told about this and given some short activities to try at home.

Other challenges

Dialect and accent

Many trainee and newly qualified teachers begin their careers in areas where their accents differ from the children they teach. For most, this is not a problem, but for some, especially when teaching phonics and spelling, this can prove challenging. Our accent is part of our heritage and helps our friends and family to identify us; for example when we phone them they will know who is calling without our having to identify ourselves. Crystal and Crystal (2014) explain that differences between accents mostly relate to the way we sound vowels, but these differences can cause confusion for pupils, for example when teaching the vowel sound in bag, pack, pass and bath. In many accents, especially in the north of England, the vowel sound is the same in all of the words (a short a), but in many accents pass and bath would have a long vowel sound, while bag and pack would have a short vowel sound. Similarly, in many accents cup and book would have similar vowel sounds, but in many accents the vowels would be sounded differently.

We are all exposed to different accents through TV and films and can almost always understand English-speaking people no matter what their accents, but for children getting to grips with grapheme–phoneme correspondences there can be confusion if, for example, a teacher who uses a long vowel sound in bath teaches in an area where the norm is to use a short vowel sound. The solution for some teachers is to modify their accents, while others make accent a topic for discussion and even tell children when teaching some vowel sounds that different people sound them in different ways. In every class there will be children with different accents, including those who are learning English as an additional language. Rather than trying to mimic the local accent, it may be better to make accent a topic for discussion so that no-one, including the teacher, feels that their speech is being denigrated.

Different schemes and programmes

A key challenge when beginning to work in a school is to become familiar with the programmes used for different aspects of the curriculum. In English, especially at key stage 1, it will be important to learn quickly the school's approach to phonics and early reading. Most schools use commercially produced programmes such as *ReadWrite Inc, Jolly Phonics* and *Sounds-Write*, or draw upon *Letters and Sounds* and adapt it for their own purposes. The good news is that most schemes have a lot in common, but all have features which may be unfamiliar to a new teacher.

The key to success is to familiarize yourself with the materials, discuss procedures with colleagues, and ask if you can observe other teachers and attend professional development courses. You can find out about the features of different programmes online and by reading texts about phonics such as Jolliffe and Waugh (2015).

Summary

In this chapter, we have shown that there are identifiable characteristics of successful teachers on English. The challenge for beginner teachers is to reflect upon their own practice and that of more experienced colleagues and consider how they can develop the qualities which will help them to enable their pupils to succeed. English is not only a core subject, but it is also at the core of the whole curriculum so establishing oneself as a successful teacher of English will be central to success across the curriculum.

From reading this chapter you should have a clearer understanding of:

- Identifiable qualities of effective teachers, with a particular focus on primary English
- Some of the challenges trainees and beginner teachers might face in primary English
- Some practical solutions to challenges.

Recommended reading

The following books are highly recommended for general reading on primary English:

Brien, J. (2012). *Teaching Primary English*. London: Sage.

Glazzard, J. and Palmer, J. (2015). *Enriching Primary English*. Northwich: Critical Publishing.

Medwell, J. and Wray, D. with Minns, H., Griffiths, V. and Coates, E. (2014). *Primary English Teaching Theory and Practice*. London: Sage.

Medwell, J. and Wray, D. with Moore, G. and Griffiths, V. (2014). *Primary English Knowledge and Understanding*. London: Sage.

Metcalfe, J., Simpson, D., Todd, I. and Toyn, M. (2013). *Thinking Through New Literacies for Primary and Early Years*. London: Sage.

Perkins, M. (2012). *Observing Primary Literacy*. London: Sage.

Waugh, D., Jolliffe, W. and Allott, K. eds. (2017). *Primary English for Trainee Teachers*, 2nd ed. London: Sage.

Waugh, D. and Jolliffe, W. (2016). *English 5-11: A Guide for Teachers*, 3rd ed. London: Routledge.

Woolley, G. (2014). *Developing Literacy in the Primary Classroom*. London: Sage.

For help with grammatical terminology:

Waugh, D., Allott, K., Waugh, R., English, E. and Bulmer, E. (2014). *The Spelling, Punctuation and Grammar app*. Morecambe: Children Count Ltd. (available through the App Store) This is an interactive app, which you can use on a smartphone and even refer to during lessons for help with explanations and activities.

The following three books provide accessible and easy-to-understand guidance on the aspects of spelling, punctuation and grammar which feature in the curriculum.

Horton, S. and Bingle, B. (2014). *Lessons in Teaching Grammar in Primary Schools*. London: Critical Publishing.

Waugh, D., Warner, C. and Waugh, R. (2015). *Teaching Grammar, Punctuation and Spelling in Primary Schools*. London: Sage.

Wilson, A. (2005). *Language Knowledge for Primary Teachers*. London: David Fulton.

For helpful video clips on grammar and the English National Curriculum see:

http://www.pearsonschoolsandfecolleges.co.uk/Primary/GlobalPages/ NewEnglishCurriculum/Debra-Myhill-Insights.aspx

For an entertaining and informative exploration of accents, see:

Crystal, B. and Crystal, D. (2014). *You Say Potato: A book about accents*. London: Macmillan.

For general guidance on different phonics programmes see:

Jolliffe, W. and Waugh, D. with Carss, A. (2015). *Teaching Systematic Synthetic Phonics in Primary Schools*, 2nd ed. London: Sage. Chapter 13.

For a guide to Letters and Sounds and useful information on systematic synthetic phonics in general, see:

DfES (2007). *Letters and Sounds: Principles and Practice of High Quality Phonics: Notes of Guidance for Practitioners and Teachers.* London: DfES.

For guidance on the principles and practice for Read Write Inc., see:

www.ruthmiskinliteracy.com and R. Miskin (2011). *Read Write Inc.: Phonics Handbook.* Oxford University Press.

For guidance on the principles and practice for Jolly Phonics, see:

www.jollylearning.co.uk/ overview-about- jolly-phonics/.

For details of Phonics Bug, see:

http://www.pearsonphonics.co.uk/PhonicsBug/OnlineReadingWorld/OnlineWorld.aspx

For information on Sounds-Write, see:

http://www.sounds-write.co.uk/

Bibliography

Aaron, P. G., Joshi, M. and Williams K. A. (1999). 'Not all reading disabilities are alike'. *Journal of Learning Disabilities, 32*: 120–37.

Adams, M. J. (1990). *Beginning to Read: Learning and Thinking about Print*. London: MIT.

Ahlquist, S. (2013). *Storyline – Developing Communicative Competence in English*. Lund, Sweden: Studentlitteratur.

Alexander, R. (2000). *Culture and Pedagogy: International Comparisons in Primary Education*. Oxford: Blackwell.

Alexander, R. (2004). *Towards Dialogic Teaching*. Cambridge: Dialogos.

Alexander, R. (2005). 'Culture, dialogue and learning: Notes on an emerging pedagogy'. Education, Culture and Cognition: Intervening for growth. International Association for Cognitive Education and Psychology (IACEP) 10th International Conference, University of Durham, UK, 10–14 July 2005.

Alexander, R. J. ed. (2009). *Children, their World, their Education: Final Report and Recommendations of the Cambridge Primary Review*. London: Routledge.

Alexander, R. J. (2012). *Improving Oracy and Classroom Talk in English Schools: Achievements and Challenges*. (Version of a presentation given at the DfE seminar on Oracy, the National Curriculum and Educational Standards, 20 February 2012).

Anderson, S. A. (1994). *Synthesis of Research on Mastery Learning*. (ERIC Document Reproduction Service No. ED 382 567).

Andrews J. (n.d). Down the rabbit hole with a handful of Apps. *NATE Teaching English. Primary English*. Available from https://www.hertsforlearning.co.uk/../nate_te_primary_matters_jane_andrews.pdf (accessed 16 January 2017).

Andrews, R. C., Torgerson, S., Beverton, A., Freeman, T., Lock, G., Low, G., Robinson, A. and Zhu, D. (2006). 'The effect of grammar teaching on writing development'. *British Education Research Journal, 32*(1): 39–55.

Assessment Reform Group (ARG). (2002). *Assessment for Learning: Ten Principles*. University of Cambridge Faculty of Education. Available from https://www.aaia.org.uk/content/uploads/2010/06/Assessment-for-Learning-10-principles.pdf (accessed 09 February 2017).

Assessment Reform Group (ARG). (2006). *The Role of Teachers in the Assessment of Learning*. Available from https://www.aaia.org.uk/content/uploads/2010/06/The-role-of-teachers-in-the-assessment-of-learning.pdf (accessed 09 February 2017).

Association of Teachers and Lecturers (ATL). (2011). Year 1 Phonics screening check. Response from the Association of Teachers and Lecturers https://www.atl.org.uk/Images/2011%20%20Y1_phonics_test_consultation_response.pdf (accessed 29 March 2017).

Ball, S. (1998). 'Performativity and fragmentation in the education economy'. *Australian Educational Researcher, 27*(2): 1–23.

Barbot, B. Besançon, M. and Lubart, T. (2015). 'Creative potential in educational settings: Its nature, measure, and nurture'. *Education 3-13, 43*(4): 371–81.

Beals, D. (1997). 'Sources of support for learning words in conversation: Evidence from mealtimes'. *Child Language, 24*: 673–94.

Bearne, E. ed. (1998). *Use of Language Across the Primary Curriculum*. London: Routledge.

Bearne, E., Grainger, T. and Wolstencroft, H. (2004). *Raising Boys' Achievements in Writing*. Baldock: United Kingdom Literacy Association.

Bearne, E., Chamberlain, L. Cremin, T. and Mottram, M. (2011). *Teaching Writing Effectively: Reviewing Practice*. Leicester: UKLA.

Bercow, J. (2008). *The Bercow Report: A Review of Services for Children and Young People (0-19) with Speech, Language and Communication Needs*. London: Department for Education.

Berger, R. (2003). *An Ethic of Excellence: Building a Culture of Craftsmanship with Students*. Portsmouth, NH: Heinemann.

Bhojwani, P. (2015). 'Multimodal literacies can motivate boys to write'. In D. Waugh, A. Bushnell and S. Neaum (eds), *Beyond Early Writing*, pp. 142–56. Northwich: Critical Publishing.

Biemiller, A. (2003). 'Vocabulary: Needed if more children are to read well'. *Reading Psychology, 24*: 323–35.

Black, P. and Wiliam, D. (1998). *Inside the Black Box: Raising Standards Through Classroom Assessment*. King's College London, School of Education (now available from NFER/Nelson).

Black, P. and Wiliam, D. (2006). *Inside the Black Box: Raising Standards Through Classroom Assessment*. London: GL Assessment Ltd.

Black, P. and Wiliam, D. (2009). 'Developing the theory of formative assessment'. *Educational Assessment, Evaluation and Accountability, 21*: 5–31.

Black, P., Harrison, C., Lee, C., Marshall, B. and Wiliam, D. (2002). *Working Inside the Black Box: Assessment for Learning in the Classroom*. King's College London, Department of Education and Professional Studies.

Black, P., Harrison, C., Lee, C., Marshall, B. and Wiliam, D. (2003). *Assessment for Learning: Putting it into Practice*. Buckingham: Open University Press.

Bloom, B. S. (1968). 'Learning for mastery'. *Evaluation Comment, 1*(2): 112.

Bloom, B. S. (1976). *Human Characteristics and School Learning*. New York: McGraw-Hill.

Bloom, B. S. (1984). 'The search for methods of group instruction as effective as one-to-one tutoring'. *Educational Leadership, 41*(8): 4–17.

Bloom, B. S., Hastings, J. T. and Madaus, G. (1971). *Handbook on Formative and Summative Evaluation of Student Learning*. New York: McGraw-Hill.

Boon, S. I. (2016). 'Increasing the uptake of peer feedback in primary school writing: Findings from an action research enquiry'. *Education 3-13, 44*(2): 212–25.

Bourke, R. (2016). 'Liberating the learner through self-assessment'. *Cambridge Journal of Education, 46*(1): 97–111.

Branson, J. and McCaughan, M. (2016). *Teaching for Mastery in English: Towards a Common Understanding*. Available from https://czone.eastsussex.gov.uk/ schoolmanagement/schoolimprovement/Documents/AWL/AWL%20conference/ Teaching%20for%20Mastery%20in%20English%20Jane%20Branson%20and%20 Mark%20McCaughan.pdf (accessed 24 October 2016).

Brien, J. (2012). *Teaching Primary English*. London: Sage.

British Film Institute (BfI). (2003). *Look Again!* Available at: http://www.bfi.org.uk/ education/teaching/lookagain/ (accessed 02 November 2015).

British Film Institute (BfI). (2010). *Using Film in Schools*. Available at: http://www.bfi.org. uk/education-research/education/education-resources (accessed 02 November 2015).

Britton, J. (1970). *Language and Learning*. Coral Gables, FL: University of Miami Press.

Brundrett, M. and Duncan, D. (2015). 'Leading curriculum innovation in primary schools project: A final report'. *Education 3-13, 43*(6): 756–65.

Bruner, J. (2002). 'Narrative distancing: A foundation of literacy'. In D. Brockmeier, R. Olson M. Wang (eds), *Literacy, Narrative and Culture*, pp. 86–93. London: Routledge.

Bryant, P. E., MacLean, M., Bradley, L. and Crossland, J. (1990). 'Rhyme and Alliteration, Phoneme Detection, and Learning to Read'. *Developmental Psychology, 26*(3): 429–38.

Burnford, S. (1963). *The Incredible Journey.* London: Puffin.

Burton, N. and Brundrett, M. (2005). *Leading the Curriculum in the Primary School.* London: Sage.

Cambourne, B. (2008). 'What can teachers do about the current debates in reading?' *Practically Primary, 13*(2): 4–5.

Cambridge Primary Review (2010). *Cambridge Primary Review.* http://www.primaryreview.org.uk

Carroll, J. B. (1963). 'A model of school learning'. *Teachers College Record, 64*(8): 723–33.

Carroll, J. B. (1971). 'Problems of measurement related to the concept of learning for mastery'. In J. H. Block (ed.), *Mastery Learning: Theory and Practice*, pp. 29–46. New York: Holt, Rinehart and Winston.

Catton, J. (2013). 'Inspiration: Cross-curricular literacy'. *English 4-11, 49*: 7–10.

CCEA (2007). *Thinking Skills and Personal Capabilities for Key Stages 1 and 2.* www. nicurriclum.org.uk (accessed 14 November 2016).

Centre for Language and Primary Education (CLPE). (n.d.). *Writing and Reading Scales.* Available from https://www.clpe.org.uk/library-and-resources/reading-and-writing-scales (accessed 14 February 2017).

Chambers, A. (1993). *Tell Me: Children, Reading & Talk*, reissue by Thimble Press, 2011.

Clark, C. (2013). *Children and Young People's Writing in 2012: Findings form the National Literacy Trust's Annual Literacy Survey.* London: National Literacy Trust.

Clarke, S. (2008). *Active Learning Though Formative Assessment.* London: Hodder Education.

Clarke, S. (2014). *Outstanding Formative Assessment: Culture and Practice.* London: Hodder Education.

Claxton, G. (2002). *Building Learning Power.* Bristol: TLO.

Close, R. (2001). National Literacy Trust. *Parental Involvement and Literacy Achievement: The Research Evidence and the Way Forward.* Slough: NLT.

CLPE. (2005). Creativity and literacy: Many routes to meaning: Children's language and literacy learning in creative arts projects. Available from https://www.clpe.org.uk/sites/ default/files/Many%20routes%20to%20meaning%20childrens%20language%20and%20 literacy%20learning%20in%20creative%20arts%20work_0.pdf (accessed 11 January 2017).

Coe, R., Aloisi, C., Higgins, S. and Major, L. E. (2014). *What Makes Great Teaching? Review of the Underpinning Research.* Project Report. London: Sutton Trust.

Coles, G. (2003). *Reading the Naked Truth: Literacy, Legislation and Lies.* Portsmouth, NH: Heinemann.

Corden, R. (2000). *Literacy and Learning Through Talk: Strategies for the Primary Classroom.* Buckingham: Open University Press.

Costa, A. L. and Kallik, B. eds (2008). *Learning and Leading with Habits of Mind: 16 Essential Characteristics for Success.* Alexandria, VA: ASCD.

Coultas, V. (2016). 'Case studies of teachers' understandings of the pedagogy of classroom talk: Some critical moments explored'. *Literacy 50*(1): 32–9.

Council for the Curriculum and Examinations and Assessment (CCEA). (2013). *Guidance on Assessment Primary.* Available from http://www.nicurriculum.org.uk/docs/key_ stages_1_and_2/areas_of_learning/Guidance_on_Assessment_Primary.pdf (accessed 13 February 2017).

Craft, A. (2002). *Creativity and Early Years Education: A Lifewide Foundation.* London: Continuum.

Cremin, T. (2010). 'Motivating children to write with purpose and passion'. In P. Goodwin (ed.), *The Literate Classroom* (3rd ed.). Abingdon: Routledge.

Cremin, T. (2015). 'Perspectives on creative pedagogy: Exploring challenges, possibilities and potential'. *Education 3-13*, *43*(4): 353–9.

Cremin, T. and Baker, S. (2010). 'Exploring teacher-writer identities in the classroom'. *English Teaching: Practice and Critique*, *9*(3): 8–25.

Cremin, T. and Baker, S. (2014). *Teachers As Writers; A PETAA Occasional Research Paper.* Sydney: PETAA.

Cremin, T. and Myhill, D. (2012). *Writing Voices: Creating Communities of Writers.* London: Routledge.

Cremin, T., Burnard, P. and Craft, A. (2006). 'Pedagogy and possibility thinking in the early years'. *Thinking Skills and Creativity*, *1*(2): 108–19.

Cremin, T. Bearne, E. Mottram, M. and Goodwin, P. (2008a). 'Primary teachers as readers'. *English in Education*, *42*(1): 1–16

Cremin, T. Mottram, M. Bearne, E. and Goodwin, P. (2008b). 'Exploring teachers' knowledge of children's literature'. *Cambridge Journal of Education*, *38*(4) December 2008: 449–64.

Cremin, T., Bearne, E., Dombey, H. and Lewis, M. (2009). *Teaching English Creatively.* London: Routledge.

Cremin, T., Goouch, K., Blakemore, L., Goff, E. and Macdonald, R. (2006). Connecting drama and writing: Seizing the moment to write. *Research In Drama in Education*, *11*(3): 273–91.

Cremin, T., Mottram, M., Collins, F., Powell, S. and Safford, K. (2009). 'Teachers as readers: Building communities of readers'. *Literacy*, *43*(1): 11–19.

Cropley, A. J. (2001). *Creativity in Education and Learning: A Guide for Teachers and Educators.* London: Kogan Page.

Crystal, B. and Crystal, D. (2014). *You Say Potato: A Book About Accents.* London: Macmillan.

Crystal, D. (2005). *How Language Works.* London: Penguin.

Crystal, D. (2006). *The Fight for English: How Language Pundits Ate, Shot and Left.* Oxford: Oxford University Press.

Crystal, D. (2012). *Spell It Out: The Singular Story of English Spelling*. London: Profile books.

Cutting, L. E. and Scarborough, H. S. (2006). 'Prediction of reading comprehension: Relative contributions of word recognition, language proficiency, and other cognitive skills can depend on how comprehension is measured'. *Scientific Studies of Reading*, *10*: 277–99.

Daly, C. (2003). *Literature Search on Improving Boys' Reading.* London: Ofsted,

Davies, N. (2013). *The Promise.* Walker Books. ISBN 9781406337280.

Davis, A. (2012). 'A monstrous regimen of synthetic phonics: Fantasies of research-based teaching 'Methods' versus real teaching'. *Journal of Philosophy of Education*, *46*(4): 560–73.

DCSF (2008a). *Teaching Effective Vocabulary: What Can Teachers do to Increase the Vocabulary of Children Who Start Education with a Limited Vocabulary?* Nottingham: DCSF Publications Ref: DCSF-00376-2008. Available from http://www.literacytrust.org.uk/assets/0002/9554/Teaching_Effective_Vocabulary.pdf (accessed 28 January 2017).

DCSF (2008b). *Talk for Writing.* Nottingham: DCSF.

DCSF (2009). *Support for Spelling.* London: DCSF.

Department of Education and Science (DES) (1990). *English in the National Curriculum.* London: Her Majesty's Stationery Office (HMSO).

DES (1975). *A Language for Life (Bullock Report)*. London: HM Stationery Office.

Desforges, C. and Abouchaar, A. (2003). *The Impact of Parental Involvement, Parental Support and Family Education on pupil Achievement and Adjustment: A Literature Review*. London: Department for Education and Skills.

Deshler, D. D. and Schumaker, J. B. (1993). 'Strategy mastery by at-risk students: Not a simple matter'. *Elementary School Journal*, 94(2): 153–67.

DfE. (2011). *Teachers' Standards*. London: DfE. Available at: www.education.gov.uk (accessed 12 December 2016).

DfE (2012). *What is the Research Evidence on Writing?* Research report DFE-RR238. London: Department for Education. https://www.education.gov.uk/publications/eOrderingDownload/DFE-RR238.pdf

DfE (2013). *The National Curriculum in England: Key Stages 1 and 2 Framework Document*. London: DfE.

DfE (2015a). *Reading: The next Steps: Supporting Higher Standards in Schools*. London: DfE.

DfE (2015b). *Carter Review of Initial Teacher Training (ITT)*. London: DFE Publications.

DfE (2015c). *Final Report of the Commission on Assessment Without Levels*. London: DFE Publications.

DfE (2016a) *Schools, Pupils and their Characteristics*: January 2016: National Tables. Available at: https://www.gov.uk/government/uploads/system/uploads/attachment_data/file/532038/SFR20_2016_National_Tables.xlsx (accessed 29 March 2016).

DfE (2016b). *National Curriculum Assessments at Key Stage 2 in England, 2016 (provisional)*. London: DfE.

DfE (2017a). 2017 Interim teacher assessment frameworks at the end of key stage 1. https://www.gov.uk/government/publications/2017-interim-frameworks-for-teacher-assessment-at-the-end-of-key-stage-1 (accessed 14 February 2017).

DfE (2017b). 2017 Interim teacher assessment frameworks at the end of key stage 2. https://www.gov.uk/government/publications/2017-interim-frameworks-for-teacher-assessment-at-the-end-of-key-stage-2 (accessed 14 February 2017).

DfEE (1998). *National Literacy Strategy Framework for Teaching*. London: DfEE.

DfES (2003). *Speaking, Listening, and Learning: Working with Children in Key Stages 1 and 2*. Ref: 0626-2003 G. Available from http://webarchive.nationalarchives.gov.uk/20110202093118/http:/nationalstrategies.standards.dcsf.gov.uk/node/84856 (accessed 18 January 2017).

DfES (2006a). *The Primary National Strategy Framework for literacy*. London: DfES Publications.

DfES (2006b). Rose, J. *Independent Review of the Teaching of Early Reading*, Final Report, March 2006. (Ref: 0201-2006DOC-EN).

DfES (2007a). *Letters and Sounds: Notes of Guidance for Practitioners and Teachers*. Norwich: DfES.

DfES (2007b) *Gender and Education: The Evidence of Pupils in England*. London: DfES.

Didau (2017). http://www.learningspy.co.uk/learning/why-mastery-learning-may-prove-to-be-a-bad-idea/ (accessed 04 January 2017).

Doherty, J. and Waugh, D. (2017). 'The wider role of the teacher'. In W. Jolliffe and D. Waugh (eds), *NQT: The Beginning Teacher's Guide to Outstanding Practice*, pp. 199–215. London: Sage.

Dombey, H. (2011). 'Distorting the process of learning to read: The "Light touch" phonics test for six year olds'. *Education Review*, 24(1): 23–32.

Dweck, C. (2008). *Mindset: How You can Fulfil Your Potential*. New York: Ballantine Books.

Education Endowment Foundation (EEF) (2017). *Improving Literacy in Key Stage Two*. London: Education Endowment Foundation.

Eisner, E. (2002). *The Arts and the Creation of Mind*. New Haven and London: Yale.

Erekson, J. A. (2010). 'Prosody and interpretation'. *Reading Horizons*, *50*(2): 80–98.

Evangelou, M., Sylva, K., Kyriacou, M., Wild, M. and Glenny, G. (2009). *Early Years Learning and Development Literature Review.* DCSF Research Report: University of Oxford.

Fernandez-Cano, A. (2016). 'A methodological critique of the PISA evaluations'. *RELIEVE*, *22*(1), art. M15. DOI:http://dx.doi.org/10.7203/relieve.22.1.8806

First Steps (2013). *Speaking and Listening Map of Development* Department of Education Western Australia. Available from http://det.wa.edu.au/stepsresources/detcms/navigation/first-steps-literacy/ (accessed 17 January 2017).

Fisher, R. (2003). *Teaching Thinking.* London: Continuum.

Fisher, R. (2005). *Teaching Children to Think and Learn* (2nd ed.). Cheltenham: Nelson Thornes.

Fisher, R. (2012). 'Talking to think: Why children need philosophical discussion'. In D. Jones and P. Hodson (eds), *Unlocking Speaking and Listening* (2nd ed.), pp. 94–107. London: David Fulton.

Fletcher, J., Grimley, M., Greenwood, J. and Parkhill, F. (2012). 'Motivating and improving attitudes to reading in the final years of primary schooling in five New Zealand schools'. *Literacy*, *46*(1).

Frith, U. (1998). 'Editorial: Literally changing the brain'. *Brain*, *121*: 1051–2.

Gardner, H. (1983). *Frames of Mind: The Theory of Multiple Intelligences.* London: Heinemann.

Gentry, J. R. (1987). *Spel ... is a Four-Letter Word.* Leamington Spa: Scholastic.

Gernsbacher, M. A., Hargraves, D. J. and Beeman, M. (1989). 'Building and accessing clausal representations: The advantage of first mention vs. the advantage of clause recency'. *Journal of Memory and Language*, *28*: 735–55.

Goddard Blythe, S. (2009). *Attention, Balance and Coordination. The ABC of Learning Success.* Oxford: Wiley-Blackwell.

Goswami, U. (1990). 'A special link between rhyming skill and the use of orthographic analogies by beginning readers'. *Journal of Child Psychology and Psychiatry*, *31*: 301–11.

Goswami, U. (1995). 'Phonological development and reading by analogy: What is analogy and what is not'. *Journal of Research in Reading*, *18*(2): 139–45.

Gough, P. B. and Tunmer, W. E. (1986). 'Decoding, reading and reading disability'. *Remedial and Special Education*, *7*: 6–10.

Gove, M. (2013a). https://www.gov.uk/government/speeches/michael-gove-speaks-about-theimportance-of-teaching (accessed 29 March 2017).

Gove, M. (2013b). Michael Gove talks about the importance of Teaching. https://www.gov.uk/government/speeches/michael-gove-speaks-about-the-importance-of-teaching (accessed 12 May 2016).

Graham, S., McKeown, D., Kiuhara, S. and Harris, K. R. (2012). 'A meta-analysis of writing instruction for students in the elementary grades'. *Journal of Educational Psychology*, *104*(4): 879.

Graham, S., Bollinger, A., Booth Olson, C., D'Aoust, C., MacArthur, C., McCutchen, D. and Olinghouse, N. (2012). 'Teaching elementary school students to be effective writers: A practice guide' (NCEE 2012-4058), Washington DC: National Center for Education Evaluation and Regional Assistance, Institute of Education Sciences, U.S. Department of Education.

Graham, S., Bruch, J., Fitzgerald, J., Friedrich, L., Furgeson, J., Greene, K., Kim, J., Lyskawa, J., Olson, C. B. and Smither Wulsin, C. (2016). 'Teaching secondary students to write effectively' (NCEE 2017-4002), Washington, DC: National Center for Education Evaluation and Regional Assistance (NCEE), Institute of Education Sciences, U.S. Department of Education.

Grainger T. (1997). *Traditional Storytelling in the Primary Classroom.* Leamington Spa: Scholastic.

Gregory, M. (2008). *Philosophy for Children Practitioner Handbook.* Montclair, NJ: Montclair State University, Institute for the Advancement of Philosophy for Children.

Guardian. (14 February 2013). *10 creative ways to teach English that deliver outstanding results* | Teacher Network | The Guardian.html (accessed 29 March 17).

Güngör, A. (2008). 'Effects of drama on the use of reading comprehension strategies and on attitudes towards reading'. *Journal for Learning Through the Arts, 4*(1): 1–30.

Gunther, R. (1997) *Before Writing: Rethinking the Paths to Literacy.* London: Routledge.

Guskey, T. (1990). 'Cooperative mastery learning strategies'. *The Elementary School Journal, 91*(1): 33–42.

Guskey, T. (2010). 'Lessons of mastery learning'. *Educational Leadership Interventions That Work, 68*(2): 52–7.

Guskey, T. R. and Pigott, T. D. (1988). 'Research on group-based mastery learning programs: A meta-analysis'. *Journal of Educational Research, 81*: 197–216.

Hardman, F., (2011). 'Promoting a dialogic pedagogy in English teaching'. In J. Davison, C. Daly and J. Moss (eds), *Debates in English Teaching*, pp. 36–47. Oxon: Routledge.

Harris, A. and Goodall, J. (2007). *Engaging Parents in Raising Achievement – Do Parents Know they Matter?* Research Report DCSF RW004. London: DCSF.

Hattie, J. (2009). *Visible Learning: A Synthesis of Over 800 Meta-Analyses Relating to Achievement.* London: Routledge.

Hattie, J. (2012). *Visible Learning for Teachers: Maximizing Impact on Learning.* London: Routledge.

Hendy, M. (2016). 'The promise of a picture book'. *English 4-11, 57*: 5–8.

Higgins, S. (2013). 'What can we learn from research?' In Waugh, D. and Neaum, S. *Beyond Early Reading.* Northwich: Critical Publishing.

Higgins, S. (2015). 'Research-based approaches to teaching writing'. In Waugh, D., Bushnell, A. and Neaum, S. (eds), *Beyond Early Writing.* Northwich: Critical Publishing

Hillocks, G. (1986). *Research on Written Composition: New Directions for Teaching.* Urbana IL: National of Teachers of English.

Howe, A. (1993). 'Perspectives on oracy'. In S. Brindley (ed.), *Teaching English*, pp. 38–47. London: Routledge.

Hunt, G. (2001). Raising awareness of grammar through shared writing. In J. Evans (ed.) *The Writing Classroom: Aspects of writing and the primary child 3-11.* London: David Fulton.

Hutchins, P. (1967). *Rosie's Walk.* New York, NY: Simon & Schuster Books for Young Readers.

Ings, R. (2010). *Writing is Primary: Action Research on the Teaching of Writing in Primary Schools.* Esmée Fairburn Foundation

Isakson, C. S. and Spyridakis, J. H. (2003). 'The influence of semantics and syntax on what readers remember'. *Technical Communication, 50*(4): 538–53.

Jeffrey, B. (2006). 'Creative teaching and learning: Towards a common discourse and practice'. *Cambridge Journal of Education, 36*(3): 399–414.

Jenkins, J., Antil, L., Wayne, S. and Vadasy, P. (2003). 'How cooperative learning works for special education and remedial students'. *Exceptional Children, 69*: 279–92.

Johnson, D. W. and Johnson, F. P. (2000). *Joining Together: Group Theory and Group Skills* (6th ed.). Boston, MA: Allyn and Bacon.

Johnson, D. W. and Johnson R. (1985). 'Internal dynamics of cooperative learning groups'. In R. Slavin, S. Sharan, S. Kagan, R Hertz-Lazarowitz, C. Webb and R. Schmuck (eds), *Learning to Cooperate: Cooperating to Learn*, pp. 103–24. New York: Plenum Press.

Johnson, D. W. and Johnson, R. (1989). *Cooperation and Competition: Theory and Research.* Edina, MN: Interaction Book Company.

Johnson, D. W. and Johnson, R. T. (1999). *Learning Together and Alone: Cooperation, Competitive and Individualistic Learning* (5th ed.). Boston, MA: Allyn & Bacon.

Johnson, D. W. and Johnson, R. T. (in press). 'The use of cooperative procedures in teacher training'. *Journal of Education for Teaching, 43*(1).

Jolliffe, W. (2007). *Cooperative Learning in the Classroom: Putting it in Practice*. London: Sage.

Jolliffe, W. (2015). 'Bridging the gap: Teachers cooperating together to implement cooperative learning'. *Education 3-13, 43*(1): 70–82.

Jolliffe, W. and Waugh, D. with Carss, A. (2015). *Teaching Systematic Synthetic Phonics in Primary Schools* (2nd ed.). London: Sage.

Jones, D. (2017). 'Talking about talk: Reviewing oracy in English primary education'. *Early Child Development and Care, 187*(3–4): 498–508.

Joyce, B. R., Weil, M. and Cahoun, E. (2014). *Models of Teaching* (9th ed.). London: Pearson.

Kagan, S. (1994). *Cooperative Learning*. San Juan Capistrano, CA: Kagan Cooperative Learning.

Kennedy, R. (2014). 'Being authors: Grammar explanation'. *English 4-11*. Spring 2014: 2–4.

King, S. (2001). *On Writing: A Memoir of the Craft*. London: New English Library.

Kintsch, W. A., and van Dijk, T. A. (1978). 'Toward a model of text comprehension and production'. *Psychological Review, 85*: 363–94.

Kintsch, W. A., Welsch, D., Schmalhofer, F. and Zimny, S. (1990). 'Sentence memory: A theoretical analysis'. *Journal of Memory and Language, 29*: 133–59.

Kispal, A. (2008). *Effective Teaching of Inference Skills for Reading: Literature Review*. DCSF Research Report (031). London: DCSF.

Krathwohl, D. R. (2002). 'A revision of Bloom's taxonomy: An overview, theory into practice'. *Theory into Practice, 41*(4): 212–18.

Kress, G. R. (1997). *Before Writing: Rethinking Paths to Literacy*. London: Routledge.

Kress, G. R. (2003). *Literacy in the New Media Age*. London: Routledge.

Kress, G. R. and Van Leeuwen, T. (2006). *Reading Images: The Grammar of Visual Design* (2nd ed.). London: Routledge.

Kuhn, M., Schwanenflugel, P. J., Morris, R. D., Morrow, L. M., Gee Woo, D., Meisinger, E. B., Sevcik, R. A., Bradley, B. A., Stahl, S. A. (2006). 'Teaching children to become fluent and automatic readers'. *Journal of Literacy Research, 38*(4), 357–87.

Kulik, C. C., Kulik, J. A. and Bangert-Drowns, R. L. (1990). 'Effectiveness of mastery learning programs: A meta-analysis'. *Review of Educational Research, 60*: 265–99.

Kyndt, E., Raes, E., Lismont, B., Timmers, F., Cascallar, E. and Dochy, F. (2013). 'A meta-analysis of the effects of face-to-face cooperative learning. Do recent studies falsify or verify earlier findings?' *Educational Research Review 10*: 133–49.

Lane, S. (1980). *The Art of Maurice Sendak*. London: Bodley Head.

Libraries All Party Parliamentary Group. (2014). *The Beating Heart of the School, Improving Educational Attainment Through School Libraries and Librarians*. London: Chartered Institute of Library and Information.

Lipman, M. (2003). *Thinking in Education* (2nd ed.). Cambridge: Cambridge University Press.

Littleton, K. and Mercer, N. (2013). *Interthinking: Putting Talk to Work*. Abingdon: Routledge.

Luke, A. and Freebody, P. (1999). 'A map of possible practices: Further notes on the four resources model'. *Practically Primary, 4*: 5–8.

Luoma, S. (2004). *Assessing Speaking*. Cambridge: Cambridge University Press.

McGuinness, D. (2004). *Early Reading Instruction: What Science Really Tells us About How to Teach Reading*. Cambridge, MA: MIT Press.

Medwell, J. and Wray, D. (2007) 'Handwriting: What do we know and what do we need to know?' *Literacy 41*(1): 10–15.

Medwell, J., Wray, D., Poulson, L. and Fox, R. (1998). *Effective Teachers of Literacy*. http://www.leeds.ac.uk/educol/documents/000000829.htm#ch3 (accessed 27 March 2017).

Mercer, N. (2000). *Words and Minds: How we Use Language to Think Together.* London: Routledge.

Merisuo-Storm, T. (2006). 'Girls and boys like to read and write different texts'. *Scandinavian Journal of Educational Research*, 50, No. 2 April metalinguistic understanding', *Research Papers in Education, 27*(2): 139–66.

Meyer, B. J. F. (1984). 'Text dimensions and cognitive processing'. In H. Mandl, N. L. Stein and T. Trabasso (eds), *Learning and Comprehension of Text*, pp. 3–51. Hillsdale, NJ: Lawrence Erlbaum Associates.

Myhill, D. (2006). 'Talk, talk, talk: Teaching and learning in whole class discourse'. *Research Papers in Education, 21*(1): 19–41.

Myhill, D., Lines, H. and Watson, A. (2011). *Making Meaning with Grammar: A Repertoire of Possibilities*. Exeter: University of Exeter.

Myhill, D. A., Jones, S. M., Lines, H. and Watson, A. (2012). 'Re-thinking grammar: The impact of embedded grammar teaching on students' writing and students' metalinguistic understanding'. *Research Papers in Education, 27*(2): 139–66.

NALDIC (1999). Working Paper 5: *The Distinctiveness of EAL: A Cross-Curricular Discipline*. Watford: NALDIC

NALDIC (2013). *Maintained Primary and Secondary Schools: Number and Percentage of Pupils by First Language*. Available at: http://www.naldic.org.uk/Resources/NALDIC/Research%20and%20Information/Documents/Copy%20of%20EALpupils19972013.xls (accessed 3 December 2016).

National Association of Advisers in English (NAAE), The National Association for the Teaching of English (NATE) and the United Kingdom Literacy Association (UKLA) (2015). *Curriculum and Assessment in English 3 to 19: A Better Plan*. Available from https://ukla.org/downloads/Summary_and_Introduction.pdf (accessed 15 February 2017).

National College for Teaching and leadership (NCTL) (2014). *Beyond Levels: Alternative Assessment Approaches Developed by Teaching Schools. Research Report*. https://www.gov.uk/government/uploads/system/uploads/attachment_data/file/349266/beyond-levels-alternative-assessment-approaches-developed-by-teaching-schools.pdf (accessed 13 February 2017).

National Teacher Research Panel, *Practitioner Summary* (2010). http://www.ntrp.org.uk/sites/all/documents/A.%20Price%20FINAL.pdf. (accessed 28 March 2017).

NCSL (2007). *Lifting the Lid on the Creative Curriculum*. Available from http://dera.ioe.ac.uk/7340/1/download%3Fid%3D17281%26filename%3Dlifting-the-lid-on-the-creative-curriculum-full-report.pdf. (accessed 09 January 2017).

Norman, K. ed. (1992). *Thinking Voices: The Work of the National Oracy Project*. London: Hodder & Stoughton.

O'Riordan, N. J. (2016). 'Swimming against the tide: Philosophy for children as counter-cultural practice'. *Education 3-13, 44*(6): 648–60,

O'Sullivan, O. and McGonigle, S. (2010). 'Transforming readers: Teachers and children in the Centre for Literacy in Primary Education Power of Reading project'. *Literacy, 44*(2): UKLA 51–59.

Oakhill, J. V. and Cain, K. (2012). 'The precursors of reading ability in young readers: Evidence from a four-year longitudinal study'. *Scientific Studies of Reading, 16*(2): 91–121.

Oatley, K. (2008). *The Mind's Flight Simulator*. Available at: www.thepsychologist.org.uk/archive/archive_home.cfm?volumeID=21&editionID=167&ArticleID=1441 (accessed 10 March 2017).

Ofsted (2005). *English 2000–2005: A Review of Inspection Evidence.* London: Ofsted.

Ofsted (2007). *Poetry in Schools: A Survey of Practice, 2006/07.* London: Ofsted. http://www.ofsted.gov.uk/resources/poetry-schools (16 June 2014).

Ofsted (2009a). *Twenty Outstanding Primary School: Success Against the Odds.* Manchester: Ofsted.

Ofsted (2009b). *English at the Crossroads: An Evaluation of English in Primary and Secondary Schools 2005–8.* London: HMSO.

Ofsted (2010) *Learning: Creative Approaches that Raise Standards.* Ofsted Publications available from http://www.creativitycultureeducation.org/learning-creative-approaches-that-raise-standards (accessed 16 January 2017).

Ofsted (2016). *School Inspection Handbook: Handbook for Inspecting Schools Under Section 5 of the Education Act 2005.* London: Ofsted.

Oke, J. and Oke, J. (2004) *Naughty Bus.* Little Knowall. ISBN 9780954792114.

Pantaleo, S. (2015). 'Language, literacy and visual texts'. *English in Education,* (2): 113–29.

PIRLS (Progress in International Reading Literacy Study) (2006). *Readers and Reading: National Report for England 2006.* Twist, L., Schagen, I. and Hodgson, C. of London: National Foundation for Educational Research.

Prais, S. J. (2003) 'Cautions on OECD's Recent Educational Survey (PISA)'. *Oxford Review of Education,* 29(2): 139–63.

Primary National Strategy and United Kingdom Literacy Association (PNS/UKLA) (2004). *Raising Boys' Achievements in Writing.* London: PNS/UKLA.

QCA (2005). *Creativity find it! Promote it! - Promoting Pupils' Creative Thinking and Behaviour Across the Curriculum at Key Stages 1, 2 and 3 – Practical Materials for Schools.* London: QCA.

Qualifications and Curriculum Authority (QCA)/Department for Education and Science (DfES) (2003). *New Perspectives on Spoken English in the Classroom.* London: QCA.

Quigley, A. (2013). http://www.theconfidentteacher.com/2013/03/shared-writing-modelling-mastery/ (accessed 31 January 2017).

Rasinski (n.d.). http://www.timrasinski.com/presentations/IRA07Tim_Rasinski_2.pdf (accessed 27 January 2017).

Reedy, D. and Bearne, E. (2013). *Teaching Grammar Effectively in Primary Schools.* Leicester: UKLA.

Rooke, J. (2013). *Transforming Writing: Final Evaluation Report.* London: National Literacy Trust.

Rose, J. (2009). *Independent Review of the Primary Curriculum: Final Report.* Nottingham: DCSF.

Rosenshine, B. (2010). Principles of Instruction. International Academy of Education, UNESCO. Geneva: International Bureau of Education. http://www.ibe.unesco.org/fileadmin/user_upload/Publications/Educational_Practices/EdPractices_21.pdf

Roth, K. and Guinee, K. (2011). 'Ten minutes a day: The impact of interactive writing instruction on first graders' independent writing'. *Journal of Early Childhood Literacy,* 11(3): 331–61.

Sach, E. (2015). 'An exploration of teachers' narratives: What are the facilitators and constraints which promote or inhibit "good" formative assessment practices in schools?' *Education 3-13,* 43(3): 322–35.

Sadler, R. (1989). 'Formative assessment and the design of instructional systems'. *Instructional Science,* 18: 119–44.

Safford, K. (2016). 'Teaching grammar and testing grammar in the english primary school: The impact on teachers and their teaching of the grammar element of the statutory test in Spelling, Punctuation and Grammar (SPaG)'. *Changing English,* 23(1): 3–21.

Scarborough, H. S. (2001). 'Connecting early language and literacy to later reading (dis) abilities: Evidence, theory, and practice'. In S. Neuman and D. Dickinson (eds), *Handbook for Research in Early Literacy*, pp. 97–110. New York: Guilford Press.

Sendak, M. (1992). *Where the Wild Things Are*. London: HarperCollins.

Sharan, S. (1990). *Cooperative Learning: Theory and Research*. Westport, CT: Praeger.

Siraj-Blatchford, I., Shepherd, D.-L., Melhuish, E., Taggart, B., Sammons, P., Sylva, K. (2011). *Effective Primary Pedagogical Strategies in English and Mathematics in Key Stage 2: A study of Year 5 classroom practice drawn from the EPPSE 3-16 longitudinal study*. London: DfE.

Slavin, R. E. (1986). *Using Student Team Learning* (3rd ed.). Baltimore, MD: Johns Hopkins University Press.

Slavin, R. E. (1995). *Cooperative Learning: Theory, Research, and Practice*. Boston: Allyn & Bacon.

Stuart, M. and Stainthorp, R. (2016). *Reading Development and Teaching*. London: Sage.

Sutton Trust (2017). The Evidence Endowment Foundation: Teaching and Learning Toolkit: https://educationendowmentfoundation.org.uk/resources/teaching-learning-toolkit/ (accessed 09 February 2017).

Swaffield, S. (2008). *The Misrepresentation of Assessment for Learning – and the Woeful Waste of a Wonderful Opportunity*. Paper presented at the 2009 AAIA National Conference (Association for Achievement and Improvement through Assessment) Bournemouth, 16–18 September 2009.

Tan, S. (2007). *The Arrival*. London: Hodder Children's Books.

Tilstra, J., McMaster, K., Van den Broek, P., Kendeou, P. and Rapp, D. (2009). 'Simple but complex: Components of the simple view of reading across grade levels'. *Journal of Research in Reading*, *32*: 383–401.

Topping, K. Duran, D. and Van Keer H. (2016). *Using Peer Tutoring to Improve Reading Skills: A Practical Guide for Teachers*. Abingdon: Routledge.

Topping, K. J. (2009). 'Peer assessment'. *Theory into Practice*, *48*(1): 20–27.

Topping, K. J. (2010). 'Methodological quandaries in studying process and outcomes in peer assessment: Commentary'. *Learning and Instruction*, *20*(4): 339–43.

Trickey, S. and Topping, K. J. (2004). 'Philosophy for children: A systematic review'. *Research Papers in Education*, *19*(3): 365–80.

Tripp, D. (1993). *Critical Incidents in Teaching*. Abingdon, OX: Routledge.

Trzebiatowski, K. (2017). 'Building academic language in learners of english as an additional language: From theory to practical classroom applications'. In W. Jolliffe and D. Waugh (eds), *NQT: The Beginning Teacher's Guide to Outstanding Practice*, pp. 143–64. London: Sage.

Tunmer, W. E. and Chapman, J. W. (2012). 'The simple view of reading redux: Vocabulary knowledge and the independent components hypothesis'. *Journal of Learning Disabilities*, *45* (5): 453–66.

Twist, L., Schagen, I. and Hodgson, C. (2007). *Readers and Reading Progress in International Reading Literacy Study: National Report for England*. Slough: NFER.

UKLA (2004). *Raising Boys' Achievements in Writing*. Royston: UKLA.

U.S. Department of Education, Institute of Education Sciences, National Center for Education Statistics, National Assessment of Educational Progress (NAEP) (2002). Oral Reading Study.

Vadasy, P. F., Sanders, E. A. and Herrera, B. L. (2015). 'Efficacy of rich vocabulary instruction in fourth- and fifth-grade classrooms'. *Journal of Research on Educational Effectiveness*, *8*(3): 325–65.

Vockell, E. L. (1993). 'Why schools fail and what we can do about it'. *Clearing House*, *66*(4): 200–5.

Vygotsky, L. V. (1978). *Mind in Society: The Development of Higher Psychological Processes*. Cambridge, MA: Harvard University Press.

Vygotsky, L. S. [y1931] (1991). 'Imagination and creativity in the adolescent'. *Soviet Psychology, 29*: 73–88.

Vygotsky, L. S. (2004 [1930]). 'Imagination and creativity in childhood'. (Trans. F. Smolucha). *Journal of Russian and East European Psychology, 42*(1): 7 –97.

Warner, C. (2017). 'Writing'. In D. Waugh, W. Jolliffe and K. Allott (eds), *Primary English for Trainee Teachers*. London: Sage.

Washburne, C. W. (1922). 'Educational measurements as a key to individualizing instruction and promotions'. *Journal of Educational Research, 5*: 195–206.

Waugh, D. (2015). 'How Danny the champion of the world saved my career' TeachPrimary. http://www.teachprimary.com/learning_resources/view/how-danny-the-champion-of-the-world-saved-my-career (accessed 6 April 2017).

Waugh, D., Warner C. and Waugh R. (2016). *Teaching Grammar, Punctuation and Spelling in Primary Schools* (2nd ed.). London: Sage.

Waugh, D., Sanderson, R., McMahon, E., Stewart, I., Kay, A., Joyce, F., Armstrong, G., Hood, A., Martin, E., Wood, T., Gibbins, I., Atkinson, I., English, B., Appleby, S., Halsall, F., Pearson, A., Harris, A., Dawson, G., Fisher, A., Waistell, R., Semple, K., Hird, E., Fortune, H., Boxall, L., Swan-Learoyd-Ashmain, S., Watkins, E., Ramage, L., Mawson, L., Frater, C., Rutter-Bryson, H., Gilling, P., Robinson, C., Elves, J., Humphries, A., Robson, N., Wilson, B., Moore, D., Myers, A., Blair, T., Dawson, B., Crane, D., Nicholson, A., Cooper, V., Watt, P., Colles, M., Pierce, J., Piercy, H. and Taylor, G. (2017). *The Wishroom*. Bishop's Castle: Constance Books.

Westgate, D. and Hughes, M. (2015). 'Speaking and listening across the primary curriculum: An entry to improved learning and a focus for CPD'. *Education 3-13, 43*(5): 565–78

Westgate, D. and Hughes, M. (2016). 'Speaking and listening in the primary curriculum: Some themes and their impact'. *Education 3-13, 44*(4): 478–95.

White, T. G., Graves, M. F. and Slater, W. H. (1990). 'Growth of reading vocabulary in diverse elementary schools: Decoding and word meaning'. *Journal of Educational Psychology, 82*: 281–90.

Whitehead, M. (2007). *Developing Language and Literacy with Young Children*. London: Paul Chapman.

Whybrow, I. (1995). *Little Wolf's Book of Badness*. London: Harper Collins Children's Books.

Wiliam, D. (2000). 'Formative assessment in mathematics part 3: The learner's role'. Equals: *Mathematics and Special Educational Needs, 6*(1): 19–22.

Wiliam, D. (2011a) *Embedded Formative Assessment*. Bloomington, IN: Solution Tree Press.

Wiliam, D. (2011b). 'What is assessment for learning?' *Studies in Educational Evaluation, 37*(1): 3–14.

Wiliam, D. (2012) 'Think you've implemented assessment for learning?' *Times Educational Supplement 13 July 2012.*

Woolley, G. (2014). *Developing Literacy in the Primary Classroom*. London: Sage.

Wray, D., Medwell, J., Poulson, L. and Fox, R. (2003). *Teaching Literacy Effectively in the Primary School.* London: Routledge.

Wylie, R. E. and Durrell, D. D. (1970). 'Teaching vowels through phonograms'. *Elementary English, 47*: 787–91.

Index

activating prior knowledge 93
alphabetic code 86–7
assessment 129–43
    curriculum progression objectives 138
    feedback 130
    formative assessment 129, 131–4
    forms of 131
    interim assessment levels 136–7
    mastery statements 138
    peer and self-assessment 139–41
    revised Bloom's taxonomy 138
    schools approaches 137–9
    summative assessment 134–5
    visible learning approaches 137–8
    without levels 135–9
assessment for learning 20

Centre for Literacy in Primary
    Education (CLPE) 39, 54
    Reading and Writing Scales 139
challenges for trainee and beginner teachers
    12–13, 145–63
classroom climate 151–6
classroom management 146, 157–9
common exception words 88
composition skills 103–5
comprehension 84
    language comprehension 84, 90
    linguistic comprehension 84
content or subject knowledge 147
cooperative learning 21, 26–7
    cooperative group work 81–2
creative approaches 33–49
creative partnerships 34
creativity 34–5
cross-curricular teaching 11–12

decoding 84
dialects 14, 162–3
    dialect and accent 162–3
dialogic teaching 82
differentiation 149–50
digital texts 58

displays 55–6
drama 42

Education Endowment Foundation 15, 21
effective ways to teach literacy 7–8, 150–1
English as an additional language 6, 16
English orthography 12
enjambement 63

feedback 23, 24, 28, 30
fiction 56–7
film 46–7
fluency 88–90
    strategies for fluency 89
formative assessment 109
four modes of language 9–10

grammar 101–3, 148
grapheme/phoneme correspondences 13

handwriting 99–100

immersive social learning 48–9
inference skills 93–4
    teaching strategies 95
    type of inference 94

libraries 55
LINC 20
literacy wars 6
literature portfolio 66–70
look and say 88

mastery and cooperative learning 26–7
Mastery in National Curriculum 22
mastery learning 20–2, 24–5
    classroom approaches 28–30
modelling 63
multi-modality 6

National Curriculum 19, 34, 73
National Literacy Strategy 10
National Oracy Project 10

neuroscience   5
non-fiction   58
    non-fiction genres   58, 120
    varieties of non-fiction   120

oracy   9, 10

pace and timing   149
peer critique   23–4, 141
philosophy for children   79–80
phonemes   12
phonics   13, 19
    effective teaching of phonics   87
    International Phonetic Alphabet   86
    phonics screening check   14
    role of phonics   85
PIRLS   51–2
PISA   19
play   40–1
poetry   61–3
    advertising jingles   63
    comic verse   64
    free verse   63, 64
    narrative poetry   63, 64
    nonsense poems   64
    nursery rhymes   63
    rhyming mnemonics   64
    song lyrics   63
    syllabic patterns   64
primary curriculum   13–15
professional behaviours   160–1
punctuation   100–1, 148

QCA   10, 34

reading clubs   54
reading events   54
reading for pleasure   53–6
reading opportunities   65
reading to children   57–8
relevance, control, ownership and
        innovation   36–8
rimes   12

schemes and programmes   163
semantic skills   92–3
sight vocabulary   88
Simple View of Reading   84, 91

SPAG   13
speaking and listening   74–8
    progression   75–6
    teaching strategies   76–8
spelling   97–9
spoken language   10
standard English   14
storyline   43–4
storytelling   41–2
syntax   92, 148
systematic synthetic phonics   19

take one picture   46
talk   41–2
talk for writing   41, 109
teachers as readers   65–6
teachers as writers   122–5
teachers' beliefs   159–60
teaching-and-learning-toolkit   15, 21
technology   47–8
transcription skills   97
twenty-first century skills   34

usage   149

visual texts   45–6
vocabulary   90–1

word recognition   84–5
writing   96, 107
    characters   118
    collections   118
    dialogue   119
    gender gap   115–16
    grammar and writing   125–7
    guided writing   108
    modelling writing   107
    picture books   119
    progress in writing   114–15
    settings   118
    shared writing   28, 108, 110–12
    story openings   118
    strategies for writing   112–13
    teacher as scribe   107
    teaching approaches   108
    text genres   116
    writing with and for
        children   121